"**When Love speaks, the voice of all the gods makes heaven drowsy with the harmony**" - Shakespeare

"**It is the mark of an educated mind to be able to entertain a thought without accepting it**" - Aristotle

"Thou carriest within thee a sublime Friend whom thou knowest not. For God dwells in the inner part of every man, but few know how to find Him. The man who sacrifices his desires and his works to the Beings from whom the principles of everything stem, and by whom the Universe was formed, through this sacrifice attains perfection. For one who finds his happiness and joy within himself, and also his wisdom within himself is one with God. And, mark well, the soul which has found God is freed from rebirth and death, from old age and pain, and drinks the water of Immortality." - Bhagavad-Gita

Twin Flames, Merkabas' and More.

A Lightworkers story

www.imetatron.com

Dedicated to

Everyone's Mum

Let us make her proud

So what is all of this Twin Flame stuff about? What is a lightworker, or a Merkaba? And what makes me qualified to talk about any of it?

I am Robbie Mackenzie, a trance medium. And some years ago I channeled a book called 'Metatron, this is the Clarion call'. It describes lightworkers, the twin flame connection, what a Merkaba is and how to open it. And how, once you meet your Twin Flame, your romantic life changes into a sacred, divine experience. The likes of which you can have with no-one else. But here's the sticky bit. It brings up all that you need to deal with within yourself. EVERYTHING. And if you are prepared to face yourself and clear out all the debris that is keeping you from your divine center, the reward is a magnificent, abundant, passionate and fun life together that is the fulfillment of all that you could ever wish for in a romantic connection.

There is a deeper meaning to why Twin Flames and soul mates are connecting just now. The love that they spark together is vital for the shift in consciousness that is happening. The Romance, Tantra, and fun you have together are important to help the World ascend.

This is an account of my life, how I became a medium, met my Twin Flame Angelina, the books that I have channeled, and what ascension is all about. I hope it benefits your path and you enjoy reading it.

Best wishes,

Robbie Mackenzie

In the beginning

I was aware of interacting with other dimensions for as long as I can remember. As a child under seven, I experienced sexual abuse from a family member and for a long time blanked out many parts of the first years of my life. Despite this, my early childhood wasn't bad. I had loving parents that had a very biblical perspective on discipline and my Father was a strict disciplinarian. This had its good side and its hard side. On the positive side, it has helped create in me a very polite and considerate person, especially with regards to cursing. I have an enhanced antenna about who I am around that can take any kind of crudity in my jokes and expression, and who can't. Some of my earliest memories were of being held down, having my teeth forcibly brushed with soap and water after being heard repeating some forbidden profanity. And my Father, upon finding out about some wrong-doing, telling me to go upstairs, pull my trousers and pants down and bend over the bed to await the belting that he would be giving me. "And if you are not in that position when I come up - you will get double." He would say, slowly and menacingly. And he meant it, as I found out many times. I remember being 'Extra' bad several times and the punishment was a whole weekend spent in complete darkness in my room from the time I arrived back from school on Friday, till Monday morning with the windows blacked out, not allowed to make a sound. There were no Facebook or video games for me in those days. I have justified this to myself many times by reasoning that I probably deserved it as I could be a cheeky wee smartarse and was a very hyperactive kid. I would have probably got the label of ADHD if I had been born later. But upon deeper reflection, I think my dad could be far too over zealous in this regard. And the degree of his anger was not justifiable. I never hit him back and his punishments increased the older I got. This makes him sound like a terrible person. But the truth is he really believed he was 'Correcting' me. My brother received the same treatment, though he was much gentler on my wee sister. Boys were meant to be tough in his opinion, so he tried to toughen us up. She did get his psychological punishments though. Nobody escaped that. Not even my Mum.

"Whoever spares the rod hates their children, but the one who loves their children is careful to discipline them." – Proverbs 13:24

This is what my Father believed and to a certain degree, I agree with him. I don't think any child should be physically beaten though because there can be a fine line between discipline and sadism. The year I went to high school in Scotland was the year they banned corporal punishment. A development that stopped complete strangers being able to physically assault your children at their own discretion with impunity.

At age eight we moved to a new house and things were very different. We were right in front of football pitches and I couldn't be happier. The rest of my childhood was a lot easier as the abuser had been caught and cautioned, unbeknownst to me. And, though I didn't know it yet, my first girlfriend lived nearby.

When I was twelve years old, our family holidayed on a peninsula on the north west of Scotland. It was miles from anywhere and a beautiful spot. Within two hours of us arriving, my Brother and I went exploring and ended up in a wee burn (Scottish for stream) going all the way up into what seemed to me to be wild wilderness. Upon returning from our adventure, I slipped and fell on a big, sharp rock. This didn't seem like a problem at the time. As I scrambled from the bank of the stream, I limped towards the holiday house. I was obviously in shock, as I felt no pain at all. There was definitely something wrong though as I could feel my body reacting to something strange. A slapping sound and an unfamiliar wetness dripping from my leg. As I looked down I saw an open wound of maybe eight inches. My kneecap and bones protruding from the deep wound as I walked. The wetness was spurting blood and the sound was skin flapping up and down. It was only upon seeing this that I began to be alarmed. As the adrenaline kicked in, things went into slow motion. I let out the screaming wail of "MUUUUUUUUUUUUUM,"...... She was on the case in an instant and ran towards me, beckoning my Father into action stations. They wrapped my leg in towels and rushed me miles away to the nearest Doctors surgery. We were sixty miles from the nearest Hospital and the Doctor injected me with the biggest needles I'd ever seen in my life. I was more terrified of those scary needles than I was of the massive gash in my knee. He stitched me up, but instead of having x-rays ordered, he just sent me away with painkillers.

Six weeks later, I discovered, after having x-rays finally done, that the kneecap had knitted together badly. This resulted in the next few years of biopsy's and, due to a mislabeling incident, almost having my other leg amputated, instead of just the patella on the right leg. I like to think that it wouldn't have got that far but that was definitely what the sheet said, and the two older guys in my ward already had their legs amputated. Which was powerful fodder for my ever growing, introspective ponderings. I milked this for all it was worth to get out of going to school. As a result, missed almost two years of high school. This gave me a different perspective on learning because when I finally returned to school I was out of sync with everyone else. I don't believe I had a lack of intelligence. But a different perspective on my education. I was aware on some level of what the far-reaching implications of that could be. I was given official homework, but instead of focusing on it, I read books on philosophy, motivation, and spirituality. My teachers were Rumi, Dickens, Kahlil Gibran and many other people that I certainly wasn't introduced to in Auchmuty high school.

On my sixteenth birthday, I had a deep, spontaneous, transcendental experience. I felt a shift in the globe and had a feeling like somehow a significant switch had been flicked with many people, myself included. Like thousands of phone calls connecting to each other at the same time but with no loss of reception. This powerful energy continued for the next few weeks. I found out years later that this was called the harmonic convergence. A time seemingly prophesied by the Mayans that was a precursor to the end of the Mayan calendar in 2012. A global, synchronized meditation event, the first of its kind, and a profound doorway towards us having a more telepathic resonance with each other. I didn't understand the significance of this at the time. But

15

remember the important feeling of connection.

I was training in the gym a lot, experimenting with eating much less and feeling great about myself, when I started noticing girls. One girl in particular. She was a year older than me and we started dating. We were together for three years and I thought that my path was set for who I would be with in this lifetime. I was in love, hook, line, and sinker. Envisioning a life of kids, career and family barbeques uniting our families as a certainty. I couldn't see past her and we talked seriously about a life together. One night she told me she'd met someone else. She had a date with him and they kissed. She was ashen-faced with guilt. Telling me it was a mistake, and asking for my forgiveness. I forgave her, but the damage was done. I felt sick and completely heartbroken. I could not forget it. This was my first real tryst with the concept, on a real, relatable level, of what forgiveness consisted of. I said that I forgave her and tried to, but it gnawed away at me. We stayed together for another year or so but it was never the same and for years after this, I didn't trust anyone.

I became detached and a really naughty boy. Because I was blessed with a modicum of charm, I seduced many women. Not caring about their feelings at all. Seeing it as my personal crusade to lure as many women into my bed and accumulate as much experience between the sheets as I possibly could. I couldn't commit properly to anyone because I just didn't see the point. Women and emotional attachment, to me, equaled pain, and I made sure I didn't connect in that way, even though I pretended to. I learned about the technicalities of Tantra on a physical level. Ejaculation control and delayed gratification. But only on the level of making it a grand experience for the girl I targeted, so I could bring things to a great crescendo and peak experience physically. I got a kick out of it and was so detached from the inevitable emotional crescendo, that it worked perfectly for my shallow ends. I was hurt on the deepest level as far as my limited experience could understand. Every girl was her and I was determined that I wasn't going to be hurt again.

I didn't realize that this had triggered deeper trauma, caused by the earlier sexual abuse because this was my first voluntary sexual experience. I devoured everything that could bring me escape from this emotional pain. Drink, drugs, sex, violence, peak experiences that were very powerful in the moment, but never opened my heart. Self-destruction seemed to be my main goal. Skinning up joints constantly. Keeping what my Mum disapprovingly called 'Bad company' and artificially high on many things, without any emotional substance. I was under the delusion that it helped me. I told myself I was having great fun. As soon as I had to make any kind of real commitment I would just bail and move onto the next willing accomplice on my empty journey of rejection and hedonism.

This continued for many years while working as a chef, barman, and waiter mainly, with some other stuff in between in hotels up and down the country. As soon as I had my fun, got into enough trouble, and exhausted the pool of available women, I moved onto the next experience. Hotel work is seasonal, with accommodation included in many jobs, so this worked perfectly for me. This period of my life could probably fill another few books, but it's not relevant for this one.

Drama Drama Drama

When I was twenty-six I started drama-school and met a lovely girl who had almost died from being violently attacked earlier that year. Her ex-boyfriend left her for dead. And, thank God, after an almost full body blood transfusion and emergency hysterectomy she was saved. We got together and five days later, after talking about maybe going on holiday to Canada at some point, she said "You know if we go to Canada we will be staying with my Uncle, who is a minister, and he's going to want to marry us," I charmingly gestured that that might not be such a bad thing and she replied "Are you saying what I think you're saying?" I smiled and then suddenly she was on the phone to her Mum, proclaiming my proposal. Things went very rapidly after that. Her three-year-old was quickly calling me Daddy whilst running into my arms. I was truly overwhelmed and didn't want to hurt either of them. This wasn't my regular circumstance and I couldn't bring myself to pull the usual rejection maneuver I had mastered over the years. Her Dad was a church officer and a wedding was very easy to arrange. Her brother owned a kilt shop too so everything was very rapidly falling into place. My parents and sister voiced their concerns, but I dug my heels in because the horror of what they had been through weighed heavily on me and I couldn't add to their pain. So I just let it happen. It was a freight train gaining speed and deep down I knew it wasn't heading to my preferred destination, but I couldn't jump off. The wedding day came and my Dad said to me "You know Son, if you change your mind, in five years, it's okay." It seemed rather odd, but I just dismissed it and continued on with the ceremony.

We bought a house together and while we were students, worked as part-time lecturers in drama as the college employed us for the flair we showed with teaching and drama. Years passed and we became full-time lecturers after graduation. I got the Ramshorn theatre award for best student in my year and the future seemed to be set. After a while, we slept in separate rooms and though there wasn't a romantic spark between us, we had a very functional relationship, and the wee one was in a much better place. This was my first real taste of commitment since my first girlfriend. I genuinely tried to make it work and buckled down to a domestic routine. This worked fairly successfully for a few years.

During this time an event happened that would, in time, help to completely change the course of my life. I had a painful toothache for several weeks. But my dentist was unavailable until after we got back from a weeks summer holiday. I was a misery guts for most of the week. The tooth had a hole in it so big that I could fit the end of my tongue into it. I guess a filling had fallen out or something. But whatever the cause, it was really painful, despite taking strong painkillers. The week was an awful blur for me because of it.

Pontins holiday park in Wales. A six-hour coach journey either way. So for the trip back, I bought a few books to read. One of these books was called the 'Super Humans' and had different accounts of Holy men, healers, telekinesis and the like. One of the people featured was a 'Psychic Dentist'. I can't remember his name, but the story went that he used to smack people with both hands on the cheeks and repeat the exclamation "In the name of the Lord Jesus Christ, be thou whole" I was in severe pain and willing to give anything a go at that point. It wasn't a full bus. I had a double seat to myself and there was no-one looking. So I repeated the process on myself, continued reading the book, and forgot about it.

When we arrived back in Paisley I realized that the pain had completely gone and I couldn't feel a hole in the tooth anymore. I mentioned it to my wife and she said to keep the appointment with the dentist anyway as I may have just got some food stuck in it or something. A few days later the dentist confirmed that it "Had been heavily filled" that he hadn't done it, didn't know what it had been filled with. And that it was a really good job. He was a born-again Christian and as I told him the story he didn't seem surprised.

This was life-changing for me in the way I viewed the religious world. I knew that I could communicate with spirit telepathically as I had always done. But I did think I maybe just had a vivid imagination. I always vowed that I wouldn't do anything like medium-ship, evangelism or psychic stuff unless I knew it was real. Because it looked like such a sham and they seemed more interested in donations than actually helping anyone. But now I was given an event that I couldn't deny of the power of healing because the evidence was in my own mouth. It took some time to sink in. As I discussed it with different people I was met with incredulity and funny looks by some. And reinforcement of Gods power by others. On the trip to Canada, I asked my Wife's Minister Uncle his opinion about it and he said it was a "Faith builder." It was God showing me the power of healing and that I was on the right path.

On this same trip, I came face to face with my mortality and the fragility of my life. My Mum had always talked about when she visited Niagara Falls and stood on a bridge connecting the countries with one foot in the USA and one in Canada. I went to do the same thing so I could let her feel included. When I was in the middle of the bridge I had a sudden flash of despair about life and a feeling of hopelessness and helplessness. The empathic reality that I usually masked in humor or misdirection was starkly unveiled to me. I didn't even really know consciously how energetically sensitive I was at the time. A profound unveiling of how messed up the world seemed and how I was not living the life that I was meant for. But the subtle control mechanisms surrounding my life were keeping me 'in my place'. And in that second, I decided to jump. Even after the miracle of my tooth. My sensitivity was too much at this moment. Suicide was not something I had pained over or ever even contemplated before. I wasn't steeped in depression or general despair. I was usually very upbeat, optimistic and stoic in the face of life's general challenges. And yet, at that moment, the reality struck me of the senseless pain and misery in the world. That I was not living an authentic life and didn't feel I had any power to change it.

I moved to the edge and just as I committed to this final end, I felt a divine presence and the blue light of an Angel who said he was Archangel Michael. I was frozen to the spot, unable to move an inch. He told me that it was not my time and that I had much more work to do here. I had not even started yet and to not despair. I was a 'sensitive' for a reason and all would be revealed in due course. This was not my final destination and my life would be completely different within a few years. I stepped back from the edge and the presence withdrew but left me with a newfound purpose. Even though I didn't know exactly the details of what that was.

In the fifth year of our marriage, disaster struck my wife's family. Both her parents were accused of the sexual abuse of children that had been in their care several decades previously. There was a fund specifically for abused children at the orphan home where they had worked. If the person making the claim could get a conviction, they would receive over sixty thousand pounds in compensation. After the initial accusations, once the sum of money was discovered, there were many more who came forward. Some of the stories were preposterous and just didn't sound likely. We prayed a lot for them at this time. One of the girls had accused my ex-wife's mum of dragging her down the stairs by the hair and locking her in the pantry. This was a turning point for the defense in the trial. The day before this particular part was heard, by providence I believe, a picture of the pantry was discovered and they remembered that it didn't even have a door, but those seventies, multi-colored, plastic hanging blinds in place of where the door should have been. It had to be false and the lawyer presented this, which revealed the accuser as a liar. All charges against her mum were dropped. They were nearly home and dry but two of the charges stuck against her dad and he was sent down for eight years in prison. This was devastating to everyone and though I couldn't, and still don't believe that either of them was guilty, it brought up things within me that I just wanted to escape from and our marriage completely broke down very soon after that.

The Phoenix Burns

My brother got married a few months later and that was the disconnection point. I was the best man and asked her not to attend. This was a great family affair and it was almost exactly five years after my dad predicted that I might change my mind. I found out that the college was not renewing my contract, so I was out of a job. I moved in with my parents and was planning on moving to London to officially start my acting career when we found out that my mum had non-Hodgkins lymphoma, a type of cancer. This is fairly treatable when discovered early enough and the prognosis was good. We felt quite confident as the weeks went on but then discovered she also had aggressive lung cancer. This was a heavy blow and I told Mum that I would stay to help her through it. I asked my ex if she would agree to a divorce and because it was me leaving her, that she could have the house. I would just sign it over to her if she agreed to the quick split. This was a simplified divorce that can be concluded very rapidly if both parties agree to the terms and as she was getting a great deal, it was quickly decided. I had no attachment to the material side so it was a quick exit and the healing could begin. I learned on the property register later that she made a large profit from the house, which made me feel much better about the split.

I was urged to start in a meditation circle at the local spiritualist church. It was a strange mix of discovering great bliss through meditation, and sadness at my Mums situation. As time went on and we progressed through chemo and radiation therapy, the meditation became deeper.

My Mum had a lobectomy, removing part of her lung and was in the I.C.U for some time. We muddled through this, visiting her every day till she came home, hoping that they had removed it all. I had assumed all of Mums duties in the house, which was no mean feat as she was a consummate housewife. Vacuuming twice a day and dusting, dishes, washing etc. It was her great talent. And I have never seen a housekeeper so fastidious in the execution of their duties. I, on the other hand, have always been a terrible domestic monster. Messy and lazy in that regard. But I could not afford stress to be in the house. So as much as possible I toed the line and did the necessary.

I went to the gym twice a day to relieve the pressure and was guided to meditate with Moldavite on my third eye as many times as I could. I had only just discovered this high vibration stone and was blessed by the way it made me feel. I found a few meditations that showed me the Merkaba and how to activate it in different ways. The Merkaba is the geometric shape of a three-dimensional Star of David that surrounds you. Two halves of it spin in opposite directions and you activate it using your breath, visualizations, and as much love as you can allow. After a few weeks of practicing this, I was having supernatural experiences once again. This time it was me being faced with my family religions Archetype of evil - Lucifer. I was meditating on the Merkaba and feeling the bliss descending more and more when I felt an evil presence in the room. I continued doing the meditation and could feel this presence getting more and more intent on interfering with the process. This continued for almost a week and I could feel the presence when reading in the library and different times, following me home. But mostly when I was meditating in my room. It was like I was in a spooky horror film that was intent on preventing me opening my Merkaba. I didn't even know what that meant at the time but was determined to not let anything stop this. My higher-self was urging me on and I was following the guidance. It came to the night that would secure me on this path forever and I was once again doing the breath work and visualizing my Merkaba. I could feel it spinning very tangibly around me. Suddenly I heard the most stomach-churning voice at the foot of my bed whispering "Lucifer.... Luuucifer," Over and over. I could feel the evil intent and it trying to scare me by making me sense every type of evil that it wanted to do to me. And I was faced with a very clear choice between Fear and Love. I was visualizing and feeling the Merkaba spinning, ready to take off. Like I was fuelled up and ready to do a vertical take off in a Harrier jump jet. It was so palpable around me and as it got closer to what felt like an immense amount of energy. I felt the Evil coming so close that it was the trigger for my heart to fully open. My Merkaba sparked open and I was engulfed in HOLY FIRE. I expanded and exploded into it and my consciousness Ascended through all levels of awareness. I could feel every being in the World, the Universe and ALL dimensions simultaneously. Then the awareness was pure love. Everything dissolved and the illusion was no more. All there was, was love, a pure sea of divine bliss and I was this sea. I was everything and everything was me.

I had completely dissolved into the Universe. I experienced enlightenment and the breakdown of life as I had always known it. This destroyed the image of who I thought I was and showed me that we are all made from love. No matter what stage of learning this fact we are at. Everyone is divine and we shall all realize this eventually. It is inevitable and something that can only be fully appreciated experientially.

As I connected to many different masters in my meditative state, I was shown lots of things that were to come. I was told we were at the beginning of a Global transformation of consciousness that would make the world a much better place for everyone.

So what did this mean on a practical, every-day level? I wasn't suddenly walking on water or turning it into wine. I still had my personality and was having a laugh and ups and downs as always. But my capacity to deal with everything was greater. I was more balanced and willing to try to expand what I was capable of spiritually without so much incredulity. Things that I would have used previously as crutches to deal with existential angst or ennui didn't really interest me anymore. And in many ways, I felt like a newborn baby. Full of wonder and excitement at life once again.

One time as I fully opened my Merkaba, I was made aware of and empowered into a powerful healing energy through my whole body. My mum and dad were fast asleep as I was experiencing this. In coming back into my body awareness after being in the full Merkaba experience of oneness. I decided that I was going to try to completely heal my mum of her cancer. If I could do it on my tooth before I had real conviction about its efficacy, I told myself, I could do it for Cancer too. I reasoned that I wouldn't be much of a Son if I didn't at least try. I slowly walked to the foot of their bed where they were fast asleep, snoring loudly. I accessed the healing and heard a very clear and upset mum's higher self, saying "Robbie... What are you doing?" At this moment I recognized that her higher-self knew exactly what she was doing. She was a Master and had chosen this path for herself. That, from my human perspective, was hard to accept. But from the cosmic viewpoint, I knew that everything was perfect and that the coming weeks would prove to be a difficult thing for my human self.

Surgery, chemo, and radiotherapy had not proved successful and had weakened her to the point where she caught severe pneumonia. We were given a call in the early hours of the morning on the twenty-second of September saying that she had taken a turn for the worse and we should come into the hospital as she didn't have long left. This proved to be the hardest day of my life as we watched her struggling for every breath, not fully there. A few hours before she left us they took away her IV drip and all the equipment, to my brother's dismay. I asked the doctor if they could at least keep up the pretense that she had a chance for the sake of the family and they finally reinstated the equipment. I was at her side when she took her last breath in the afternoon and after a hard day of watching her struggling it was nothing short of magnificent like she had just seen heaven and her whole being looked ecstatic. I had never seen her more beautiful than in that moment. We were in crazy grief as time went fast and slow at the same time. My worst fears realized, we felt mortally wounded and experienced a deeper pain than I knew could exist. As we left the hospital the first leaves of autumn dropped. It was a late summer and once she had gone, the summer had no reason to stay. The Earth joined us in our grief and the trees shed their covering like tears dropping in sympathy with ours. Life could never be the same again as we were numb to any joy for the first time.

According to my guides, one of the greatest triumphs in this cosmic experience is when you lose someone you love. Not from the human viewpoint obviously, but from the divine perspective. We can never lose anyone really because we are eternal beings. This whole creation is set up as an experiment in making ourself believe that there are other parts of us with different personalities, dimensions and things. So the most profound and successful part of the journey is in that moment when we cannot hurt any more than we do when we believe in the pain of that separation. That grief is actually the pinnacle of the experiment. When we lose someone that we truly love, it's the most acute emotion we will ever feel in this human experience. It's not as fluffy as romantic love, or as enlightening as the oneness realization. But it is the most powerful way that we can have our hearts taken to the experience of separation. I had already experienced oneness and yet this illusion had fooled me good and proper.

The next few weeks were a surreal blur as the funeral came and went and our shattered lives were on autopilot. After a month went by there seemed to be some semblance of normality returning. Halloween approached and the kids started knocking on the door. Every year some wee wise guys jump the gun and see what they can get, days before actual Halloween. And in Scotland, you work for your candy. You tell a joke, do a dance or recite a poem etc before you get your reward. And the kids chap your door all night. My Dad always had a stack of coins and some fruit and nuts for them. He made each one work hard for it too before they got anything. If they came to the door prematurely they were chased away. This Halloween was different though as he wasn't feeling very well and didn't bother answering the door in the days running up to Halloween.

It came to the day they say the veil is thinnest between the seen and unseen worlds and my Dad had a head cold. I called the Doctor and got him some water. After a while, he came downstairs, sweating and in distress. Walking into the living room as if calculating his responsibilities and next moves, he said, out loud, but addressing himself "Right, I've brought you all up." And went back upstairs. His statement had a deep gravitas to it. Like he was directing his will towards the next stage of his journey. The Doctor arrived five minutes later and I led her up to my Dad's bedroom. As we walked in, a strange sound was coming from his throat that the Doctor said was the death rattle. That my dad was dying and there was nothing she could do. I knelt beside the bed as the last breath left his body. He was 72.

In Shock

Six weeks less three days and my Dad had joined my Mum. In silence and disbelief, I sat, totally struck dumb. I called my brother and he informed my other siblings and family. The house, at first was eerily quiet and then the kids started banging on the door and didn't stop all night, unaccustomed to our household not answering. I went over the words he said many times that night. I believe that my dad chose this exit point. He deliberately went to be with my mum. Twin flame separation was too much for him. They were the closest couple I have ever known.

"Pain facilitates transformation. It is the fertile ground where new seeds can be planted." – Metatron

This had been the most transformative year of my life. I was offered a council house in my hometown. The plan had changed. I couldn't face the acting stage and retreated into a cocoon of spiritual development. Progressing in meditation circle I noticed some of the energies as very familiar from my childhood. While the abuse took place as a child, I retreated into a safe haven in my consciousness, which had a distinctly safe feeling. I recognized this familiar essence to be my newly discovered guide 'Yashubi', an enlightened Samurai warrior. He had always been with me and it was only in times of great distress or illness when I felt his protective vibration. I started channeling him and many others. Becoming used to what it meant to be a trance medium. Distinctly different voices using me to communicate. I was pleased to help and was informed that the vibration would rise even more as time went on. I wasn't sure what this meant but was looking forward to it.

The person who abused me as a small child, broke down in tears in front of me a few weeks after my Mum and Dad died. He said that he had ruined my life and begged for my forgiveness. The majority of these memories had been suppressed for many years and this shock declaration unlocked the portion of my life that had, I believe for self-preservation, been locked away in some dusty part of my memory banks for over twenty-five years. He was terrified that I was going to reveal his pedophilic perversion and that his life would be ruined. My Mum and Dad had seemingly assured his protection. I reassured him that his secret was safe and that I would not seek retribution. I forgave him and left his house dazed and confused. In the following months and years, I dealt with the memories, anger and mixed emotion I had about my instant forgiveness. The conclusion I reached after much soul-searching and transformation, was that to say you forgive someone is to give them peace. But to forgive them truly is to give yourself peace also. I forgave him completely in my heart and the peace that came with it has helped me greatly upon my spiritual path and with counseling people who have had similar experiences.

"Forgiveness is your greatest gift in this illusion because it gives as much to the receiver as to the giver. When it is sincere, it is your pathway to freedom. Forgive everyone if you want to be free." – Metatron

I met a girl called Sally in the church meditation circle and we started dating. She had a four-year-old girl and a thirteen-year-old boy. I became a parental figure for the second time and the next few years were spent developing Spiritualist Medium-ship together and being part of a lovely wee family. After some years we figured that we were more like siblings and friends than lovers but loved each other's company anyway. Sally did a past life regression and I was in it as part of her family, as her housekeeper. I had a protective and nurturing role in her lifetimes past it seemed and after my parents passing she definitely returned the favor. We nurtured and supported each other throughout the years and I was blessed to be able to help her when her Dad passed over to spirit, several years ago. She had not had a religious upbringing but was spontaneously enlightened and went from being a total skeptic to a self-realized soul spontaneously.

As our Medium-ship increased, we were directed by spirit more and more. One weekend Sally suggested that we apply to do readings on the phone and I thought it was a great idea. Obviously led by spirit. Within a few days, we both had jobs helping people by using the spiritual gifts we had developed. This was a powerful time and I quickly realized that service was the way to let your gifts flourish. When your focus is on service, things just have a way of falling into place.

Meeting Metatron

In 2005 I channeled Archangel Metatron for the first time. This was the most powerful separate energy that I had ever encountered and he told me of many wonderful things that were to come about the ascension of mankind and that I would, after much preparation, be working on projects that would help people ascend and realize they are divine. A local medium told me that I would be connecting with Metatron and that I would channel two books with him. But I didn't expect the experience to be so intense. Metatron told me that I needed to be purified and cleansed and when the time was right that I would meet my Twin Flame. I channeled many messages from him at first but he was very clear that the fullest possible magnitude of his power able to flow through a human, safely, could only be achieved after fasting and purification. I was not exactly in the right shape for this at the time, but was very intrigued by the message with my twin flame meeting and kept it a secret.

This is a part of that channeling –

"You will meet her when the time is right. When you are at the aligned level of vibration. She will come to Scotland, and you will be two shining lights that will walk forward to help show humanity the way of relationship. And this understanding will help bring peace to the Earth. The enormity of this task will bring balance for people.

For many are not living the lives that they should be living in relationship together, in harmony, in love, in peace, and with respect. But they will. For this is the plan. There is no room for doubt. There is no room for any melancholy or any dissatisfaction, for you are on a divine mission. The Love will fill you and the light that you will become will show the way. Absorb the light, take upon yourself the truth that you are. Be free, be divine, be who you really are.

I am Metatron"

I was very happy to have foreknowledge of the relationship that would change my life. But this was all relatively new to me and I had some cognitive dissonance from the way that I had lived my life previously to suddenly being charged with a 'Divine mission!'

I kept preparing and was guided towards fasting but my efforts were not really great at first. I have always had a weight problem and my family were all big people. I believe that this stems from my childhood. Some of my early memories were of being left at the dinner table, my plate still full, not allowed to leave till I'd consumed the lot. "There are kids dying in Africa that would love to have what is in front of you" was a favorite cliché of both my parents and I just sat there wishing I could ship the plate off to those starving kids because I was stuffed. The longer this continued, however, the more ingrained the belief became that I needed three meals a day to survive. And before long I was a chubby wee kid and felt comfortable as such because that was the family standard. Recognizing these patterns has been a big factor in my transformation and though I kept being urged towards fasting, cleansing and healthy eating, the comfort of stuffing my face with rubbish, especially after my parents passing, was a thing that continued in the face of kind warnings from Metatron. Even after my enlightenment!

The wake up call for my personal discipline came to me on the seventh of the seventh, two thousand and seven. The week before this I had a dream of a nuclear bomb going off at the Doctors surgery. A few weeks previously my sister in law pointed out that I was red in the face and I felt very tired. I went to the Doctors and had blood taken and on the seventh, I was informed that I had type 2 diabetes. The doctor said that I would probably just get fatter and more ill as time went on and that I would be on medication for the rest of my life. His flippant, unsympathetic delivery of the news really took me by surprise. That was the moment that I decided that I was changing things. Metatron was my coach as I researched diabetes and the different schools of thought surrounding it. I was given an appointment with a nutritionist who gave me a prescribed NHS version of what I should eat and whilst talking with her, I asked what she thought about other leaders in her field's opinion on this condition. She had never heard of Dr. Neal Barnard MD's program for reversing diabetes, the PH Miracle diet or Dr. Richard K Bernstein's work, but was a very nice lady. I realized that if I just did what I was told and blindly followed this Nutritionist and the Doctors advice, my path was set for a very bleak future indeed.

Metatron had other ideas!

I took the pills for a fortnight and felt really ill with them. Metformin and Simvastatin was my prescription. The pills were making me see double. I felt really terrible and couldn't imagine me doing this for long. I intuitively felt that this path would lead to ultimate destruction through depression and a feeling of hopelessness. What was the alternative? Well, as Metatron had been urging me for several years now. Fasting!

So, a pure water fast or an alternative? What were my options? I looked for a way to keep my blood sugar level at as much of a constant as possible. I came across a book called the master cleanse by Stanley Burroughs. The reviews were really positive so I decided to give it a try.

The Master Cleanse is a supported fast which uses lemons, cayenne pepper and a sweetener to keep your blood sugar up. Many use maple syrup but it is just as effective with honey, and for diabetics, blackstrap molasses or agave nectar with slower release sugars. It is also important to 'keep moving' as there is no solid food consumed throughout the duration, so a senna tea or something similar with laxative effect is advised. The stuff being cleansed needs to work its way out.

<u>This book is not meant in any way to constitute medical advice. This is simply the personal account of my experience.</u>

I was advised that as this was a cleanse, that it clears negative stuff out of your system. In doing so there are a few negative effects, especially in the first few days. If you have caffeine, nicotine or any toxic substance in your system, you will have a hard time at the start, so it is advisable to stop taking anything a few days before you begin. I hadn't smoked in years and was a vegan mostly. But still loved my coffee, so it was definitely a consideration.

The people who had seen the benefits of this cleanse seemed to be raving about it. Many who had chronic illnesses were testifying to being much more comfortable. Living with greater energy and stamina and in many cases claimed that they had been completely cured!

This is nothing new to the world. Many people from the past fasted for long periods. Plato fasted for "Greater physical and mental efficiency." Aristotle, Socrates, and Pythagoras also fasted. We look to them because of their mental excellence, but they looked to fasting to get them there.

I thought lemons were acidic, but they actually alkalize the body. Alkalizing is believed by many to combat the acid problem in the body that makes us store fat to protect our organs. The idea is that although our blood pH level is kept pretty constant by the bodies natural systems, the more acidic our diet is, the harder the system has to work to retain its balance. So when our diet is taken from acidic to slightly alkaline, it starts to function more effectively. The body no longer needs to protect itself and the weight just drops off till you reach ideal weight. The Cayenne pepper is natures wonder herb. It greatly improves digestion, gives an outstanding improvement in overall circulation and strengthens the heart, arteries, and body as a whole. Some studies even say that cayenne pepper kills cancer cells!

This stimulates **Autophagy**, a process that degrades cellular components so they can be recycled. Basically cleansing and renewing the body on a cellular level. Yoshinori Ohsumi won the Nobel prize for Medicine in 2016 for his groundbreaking work on the subject. Proving what Holy books have been advocating for millennia.

I decided to go for it with this master cleanse and began the next day. This was my first attempt and I didn't make it past day one. The mixture tasted disgusting and I wasn't used to the cayenne pepper. I had a headache and felt very sorry for myself. I left it a few weeks and tried again. This time I bought cayenne pepper capsules and took one twice a day. Without the pepper, the mixture was just lemonade - very tasty. Much easier this time but I was still battling with hunger, headaches and the effect on my ego of fear. I made it to day two and gave up after someone affirmed to me that "you can not live without food." I was letting fear get in the way and was having a constant battle with my ingrained family belief system. This continued for several months but I was determined not to give up. Each time I managed to get a little further and break the chains of fear.

"God will not have his work made manifest by cowards." – Emerson.

After several months I finally made it to one week. Something changed and suddenly I felt great. I was meditating deeply and my dream state was amazing. I felt empowered and strong. My mastery was kicking in and I knew that there were bigger things ahead. It also became much easier to open and spin my Merkaba when I was cleansing.

I then took on the longest cleanse yet. 21 days and as well as being in an almost constant state of bliss, I lost quite a bit of weight. I looked like a different person in a very short period of time. This took some getting used to and my body yoyoed up and down as I got used to a new self-image. I never went back to the original big size in between cleanses but I always put on some weight. That was the part of mastering the cleanse that I really needed to work on.

I often wondered why, as a master of meditation, the Buddha had not mastered his weight. He was a big jolly chap in many of his depictions, but nobody can honestly say he was a great example of a physically healthy lifestyle.

The next few years were spent going deeper and deeper into meditation. I was cleansing, praying, purifying and channeling as much as possible and trying to follow Metatrons instructions. I had stabilized my blood sugar and was feeling healthier than I had ever felt before. Finally, Metatron told me that I was ready for the next stage of my mission. That I had purified to a sufficient degree that the fullest quotient of his power could now come through me and the books that would help transform the consciousness of mankind were ready to be channeled.

This was a very powerful time in my life. I was still getting used to such a high vibration. When Metatron came through me it was like I was being plugged into a power station and even though it had been stepped up over the years, I still hadn't experienced the full effect. He proposed a much longer fast than I'd ever done and on day 20 we were to begin the book that was going to change my life forever.

The Ascension of mankind sounded a bit grandiose. A feeling of being overwhelmed and slightly nervous came over me but I wasn't sure why. I had massive feelings of déjà vu suddenly and needed some guidance. I prayed, asking God to show me what I needed to know and almost instantly came across a quote that answered my question perfectly.

"Until one is committed, there is hesitancy, the chance to draw back. Concerning all acts of initiative (and creation), there is one elementary truth that ignorance of which kills countless ideas and splendid plans: that the moment one definitely commits oneself, then Providence moves too. All sorts of things occur to help one that would never otherwise have occurred. A whole stream of events issues from the decision, raising in one's favour all manner of unforeseen incidents and meetings and material assistance, which no man could have dreamed would have come his way. Whatever you can do, or dream you can do, begin it. Boldness has genius, power, and magic in it. Begin it now." – Goethe

I realized that I was stalling. That even though I had come a long way, I had not committed fully to the process, or put my full trust in God yet. Why? It dawned on me that the problem was the name and the different presentation of spirituality. My personal, family tradition was Christianity. And there was a certain fear about how different this path was. Even after all these years of development. I had to come back to basics and be true to my roots. This was the turning point in my life and I felt inspired by the Holy Spirit to open the Bible. It fell open at the perfect place.

Beloved, do not believe every spirit, but test the spirits to see if they are from God: every spirit that confesses that Jesus Christ has come in the flesh is from God. - I John 4:1

I fell to my knees and prayed to Jesus. I said that if there was any impurity about what I was about to do, that I didn't want anything to do with it and would give it all up right now. This was far too important and I didn't want to be responsible for a single soul being misled by any of my works and went through a divine purification in that moment. It became very clear to me that this was a holy path that I was on and I finally and fully committed to the process of my work with the divine.

The next 79 days were spent on the master cleanse. Doing the five rites yoga, chanting, praying and meditating. On day 20 we started with 'Metatron, this is the Clarion Call' and I felt amazing. Whizzing through the dimensions and was so full of holy power and energy that I finally knew for certain that the human race was going to be okay.

The words that came through me, changed me subtly with every new channeling. I had opened my Merkaba years ago and yet was being opened up more and more on so many different levels. I realized that although enlightenment can happen in an instant, that there are many different layers and levels of it. And your mastery keeps improving and developing as you commit to being in the moment and trusting your divine path. What is your divine path? The thing that excites you the most and Metatron made it very simple for me. I didn't feel weighed down with guilt like I had done sometimes in my formative religious experiences. I felt free and happy, excited and full of joy about the future. Not only for me but for everyone. The principals of this information made sense of everything that was encoded and most usually misinterpreted within the religious experience.

It also became clear that the reason that I had felt uneasy before fully committing to the Metatron book was to do with the programming that I had undergone throughout my childhood. My Grandfather was a minister and my parents were deeply religious. So I had a knowledge of the bible from an early age. Much of this was very conflicting to me in my seminal years and in discussing it with my mother many times, she too had similar concerns. I was always a big reader from early childhood and because of the family belief system, the bible was part of that literary initiation. I used the bible in a unique way. Not believing in every word with blind faith. Because I had a very acute sense of the fallibility of people since my early abuse. But using it in a synchronistic, mystical and magically divine way. I always found answers to things within the book. Even though I had to discern the meaning and avoid the violent, bigoted, and often misogynistic parts of the text. These words had, after all, been written, though I do believe many times divinely channeled, by lots of different humans. Some of them hundreds of years apart. The words that resonated with me the most were always those that spoke of God as love. The truest, most inspiring words in this holy book, to me, were in this simple passage.

Love is patient and kind; love does not envy or boast; it is not arrogant or rude. It does not insist on its own way; it is not irritable or resentful; it does not rejoice at wrongdoing, but rejoices with the truth. - Corinthians 1:13 v4

This sums up the best parts of the bible to me. I can see that all the ancient texts have a similar effect on many people in different traditions. Because being part of a family with a built in system of prescribed belief is programming and can result in an unwavering dogmatism that can hold all others in contempt. Any attempt to deviate from that belief system is seen as a betrayal of the family structure. And so it can become ingrained and perpetuated throughout the generations. This problem can only be solved through a sincere striving for truth in the face of familial, societal and peer pressure. Those that do open their eyes to the thread of truth that runs through all spiritual traditions, can end up reaping the rewards of the oneness that is true enlightenment. Once achieved, the individual can be seen energetically to hold the keys for others, because of the love that emanates from them.

In realizing this, I was set free. And the channelings became even more powerful and deep. I completed the Metatron book in the allotted time and felt amazing. The future was a wonderful dream that I had every confidence was going to manifest in alignment with my own commitment to trusting in God. I was glowing with divine power and felt like a child. Innocent once again and though I knew there was much, much more to do. I was supremely confident in all that I had been shown in those 79 days. I couldn't look at anything with eyes of judgment anymore, only revel in the magnificence of divine power.

"If you know you have something more to do with this life than simply exist. And feel a better destiny awaiting you, you are reading this for a reason.

This book, if approached with humility, will take you on a rollercoaster ride of your consciousness. It will make your life more interesting and your relationships better. Your romantic life will be much more relevant and loving and your sexual relationships much more fulfilling and exciting. It will transform your finances in a positive way and teach you how to manifest all the abundance you could ever want. Giving you the tools to be the best that you can possibly be in all areas. And approach life with passion, joy, laughter, and fun.

This is the Clarion Call for all Lightworkers." - Metatron, this is the Clarion Call

False Twin Detour

Ten minutes after I finished transcribing the Clarion Call, I connected with someone who wanted to talk about her career as a fledgling writer. I had just finished the book so could easily empathize with her

37

situation. And she was very interested in reading my manuscript. It seemed like great synchronicity and so I sent her the book to read. She was bowled over and extremely enthusiastic about promoting it. Proclaiming I was destined to be a millionaire author and that she was the key to it all. She asked me to give all my details to her assistant and she would manage my career. A businesswoman who knew the ins and outs of how to 'Be the Boss' as she put it. I already had a publishing deal and they were offering me a thousand pounds advance, so things seemed to be going in the right direction. The tone of our exchange was distinctly flirty also and I wondered if this was God directing me to the twin flame energy. But she was going to have to come to Scotland for the prophecy to be fulfilled if that was who she truly was. Just as I remembered this, an email arrived, asking for my details again, and asking if she could come to see me. She was very persistent.

She came up over a weekend but instead of it being about the book, it turned out to be all about our romantic connection and the book was hardly mentioned. I was overwhelmed and after that first weekend began traveling up and down to Manchester to see her. The energy of her situation was not all that she had made it out to be. And every different person I met there seemed to have a different view of what the reality of her life was. Everyone seemed to be romantically in love with her and she knew exactly how to play this to her best advantage. Always throwing money around. She told me that she didn't do anything by accident. I kept being told things that didn't add up and when I challenged the validity of anything that she said, I was misdirected or made to feel like I had done something wrong in even questioning her. Many different, almost deadly, dramatic things happened as I seemed to be in the underworld of the City. And she was playing all sides against each other. Mentally tied in knots, I had trusted her completely in thinking that God must have a plan for this and that if she really was my twin flame energy, that a transformation in her was bound to happen very soon.

Having given up my job as a spiritual counselor at her behest, I was training to sell insurance, also at her behest, not exactly following my passion. I was being asked to change my religion and because spiritualism can be seen as the work of the devil in her religion - the Metatron manuscript would have been buried! The publishing deal had fallen through anyway and I was being made to question my mission and what I was really here for. She wanted me to give up my house in Scotland and move to England. This was something she could not force my hand with. No matter how much she tried. I had to keep coming back to Scotland. Something within me knew that there was a good reason for this.

Feeling like my sanity was being tested, I went to see a minister who said that I was being tested by God and to keep the faith as there was always a reason for the situations we find ourselves in. I also went to see a psychiatrist to check my mental faculties. After assessing me and me relaying everything that had happened, she concluded that I was perfectly sane. That this was a stress-induced mental state. She didn't seem fazed when I told her I was a medium and was actually quite enthusiastic about the book. But she was very clear that the situation I was in was not good for me.

I was led to read several articles at the time about the Empath and Narcissist relationship. How it can be a detour on the way to the Twin Flame relationship. This certainly seemed to answer a lot of questions I had. And explained the psychological techniques that were being used. I had to trust that God had a plan for it all.

I stayed in this relationship for nine months, praying every day for guidance. After I questioned the connection between her and her friend, I was accused of being deluded and jealous. This turned out to be the final straw as she ended up becoming pregnant to him. So I finally cut all contact. **The truth always becomes clear in the end.**

I was creating all of this myself. Even though it seemed like she was doing all of the 'Negative' stuff. Everything is always a reflection of your consciousness. So I had to stay in a place of non-judgment to learn the lesson from the situation. Once again I had to come to forgiveness. This was a bit more than an adolescent kiss to overcome. This baby had saved me from this difficult situation. God had given me a gift with this pain. Once I detached and let go, my understanding of forgiveness expanded once again. And I could bless her situation from a distance.

A lot was learned from this time. How my faith in people was not always well placed. That I was far from perfect myself. But that I knew my intentions were pure. God would always bring things back to balance when I strove to follow a straight path. I had been agreeing to things against my best judgment because of the romantic idea of the Twin Flame prophecy. I came across a quote that is just perfect for this time in my journey.

"Stay close, my heart, to the one who knows your ways; relax in the shade of the tree in constant bloom. Don't stroll idly through the bazaar of the perfume-makers. Stay in the shop of the sugar-seller. If you don't find true balance, anyone can deceive you; Anyone can trick with colored straw, and make you take it for gold. Not every boiling pot is cooking what you want. Not all sugar canes have sugar. Not all abysses a peak; not all eyes possess vision. Not every sea is full of pearls." – Rumi

Divine Publicist

Having given up the quest to release the Metatron book while in this relationship, suddenly, thank God, my priorities had once again changed. I decided to self-publish and released the Clarion Call myself. I didn't have a great deal of experience with self-publishing so had to rely completely on guidance from the Angels. About two weeks after I released the book, I prayed, asking what, if anything, should I do to promote it. Within ten minutes of this prayer, I was on a Meetup site that was based in NYC. A chap had bought the Clarion Call and was opening this meetup to study and meditate with it. I should not have even been able to see this group, as he had not published it to the web yet! Metatron has a way of getting around things like that though. The group has been growing and growing, meeting up every few months or so with the help of the beautiful mother and daughter duo Taunya and Elan, and has grown to be over 800 members. None of this was my doing. I have discovered that it is much more potent to sometimes just let things evolve of their own accord with this kind of subject than to try to be a marketer.

I was told to charge $22 for the book by Metatron. It seemed like a lot of money to me and I was torn about the price. I had not started on this path to make money. I decided to go against what was said and reduced the price so that there was no profit being made from the book at all. Over the course of a few weeks, I was nagged again and again that $22 was the price and there was a good reason for this. I put the price back up and then several times took it back down to zero profit, just the cost of printing. "Know your worth" was Metatron's mantra for the next few weeks. I reduced the price again, and again, every time, even being awakened from my sleep to "know your worth, know your worth" and told that this was not just an ordinary book and neither were the ones that were to follow. This was a complete course in ascension and the ones that were ready for it were getting a great bargain. It was important to stand in my power with this issue he said because money is just an exchange of energies. That what I had done was pure and more valuable to those who would receive it with humility than any amount of money could ever pay for. Finally, I submitted and the price for every book in the series has been the same.

I asked a few friends if they would review it on Amazon. After a while, it became obvious that most of the spontaneous reviews were much more potent and enthusiastic than the ones that I had solicited. It was over a year before there was one negative review. There are well over two hundred amazing reviews now. Many people have said it is the best book they have ever read and is life-changing. I feel blessed to have been able to help people in this way and am humbled by the response. I thank God every day that I didn't let it get buried by the false twin.

After reviewing, over and over the drama of the previous year. I realized that the dark side of your consciousness was very clever and if you weren't zero pointed, you could be led astray very easily. Trust is a great thing, but blind trust in the face of evidence to the contrary is silly and not good discernment. It's not judgmental to appraise someone correctly for negative actions. I had given away my power because of believing that I was dealing with my divine compliment. But on the path towards meeting my Twin-Flame, it made me much sharper in my discernment of everyone that came across my path from then on.

Shang Po

About a month before Angelina said hello, I had a vivid, initiatic, lucid dream experience with an oriental spirit guide called Shang Po. I met him in meditation when I was first in the church circle. But he had never featured in my work or come forward in any way apart from being an observing presence, who, at certain times, I could feel.

The setting was high on the side of a mountain, in an impressive looking monastery. There were very tall spires on the top, which came to a sharp point and the drop was a stomach-churning prospect.

Since childhood, I have had a fear of heights. Up high I get a strange debilitating feeling in the back of my legs and at times feel glued to the spot, immobilized completely. Years ago I got a job as a window cleaner in Glasgow, to face and conquer this fear. I spent two years with a racing pulse and though I stopped being frozen to the spot because of having to climb a high ladder for a living, the fear never went away completely.

So here I find myself holding onto one of the tallest spires on this magnificent building. Shang Po is on a balcony, telepathically telling me to jump onto a spire that must have been twenty feet down and to the side. In between was a sheer drop of thousands of feet. No safety net here. My heart was beating ridiculously fast. I couldn't understand why I had to do this but could feel the significance of what was about to happen as being life altering. I was frozen, hanging on for grim death. The old familiar feeling was back in my legs, they were like jelly. This really seemed like the end and as I stared down into the cold, black abyss of certain death with my hands starting to slip on the icy spire I was barely gripping onto, the energy suddenly changed. I surrendered my fate to God and centered myself in deep and instant spontaneous meditation. Everything suddenly went into slow motion like when you are in a car crash and the adrenaline rush takes over. But this was different, this wasn't fight or flight. This was power and confidence like I had never experienced before. In the face of what seemed like certain death, I was in deep peace and an assured power came over me. My legs were solid and reliable and I just knew I could do it. I gripped on tight and lifted my whole body into position to jump and leaped the chasm. As I arrived at the other spire I knew I was changed. I no longer had any fear and instead of gripping onto the spire, I was suddenly balancing my whole body on the point at the top on one finger. Like I was performing in a circus trapeze act. I was flying and leaping between the spires, having such a great time.

I caught sight of Shang Po quietly waiting on the balcony and dropped down to where he stood. He looked at me and simply said "Now go, and enjoy your life as a Master"

And then I woke up.

I felt an increased weight in my expression and the way that people were reacting to me in the days and weeks that followed. There was a profound difference in the way I felt and have never been the same since that night. Mudras started making more sense as I directed energy with my intention and more easily raised kundalini in those who asked for it while doing distant healings. All of the things that the Clarion Call had promised seemed to be coming true within me. This was a turning point that couldn't be ignored.

Just after the Shang Po experience, I started talking with a girl who was very upfront about having a mental illness. She played down the extent of her condition and I didn't see why I should discount seeing her just because of this. I didn't realize exactly what I was getting myself into, but was determined by this point to tackle whatever life was throwing at me with divine trust. It was a very heart opening experience as every different scenario that she explained to me brought me into greater and greater compassion for her situation. Facebook was the medium of connection and her pictures were many years in the past. She had described herself very differently than how she looked now and had put on a couple of hundred pounds more than her pictures suggested. I could empathize as I had come from a similar experience of weight problems. I agreed to meet up with her. We were referring to each other as boyfriend and girlfriend and the night before I went down to see her, at **11:11pm**, an Angel said hello to me on Facebook.

Angelina – Hi Robbie, I'm such a big fan lol I can't wait to read your book ☺ I will order it ASAP. I really want to open my Merkaba too ☺ I love your video, It's filled with positive vibes. I must say you have an amazing angelic energy ☺ You've really inspired me on my spiritual journey <3 Thank you ☺

Robbie – Hi Angelina, I am so glad you like it ☺ I am glad you are going to get the book and open your merkaba ☺ You have a beautiful aura ☺ You will do a lot of good and help a lot of people. You have a healing and loving aura <3 It is a pleasure to connect with you ☺

I felt like I had just connected with a real-life human angel. My heart was beating out of my chest and I was more flattered than I have ever been in my life. I was being reserved because Angelina was only 23 and I had just turned 41. I thought that she was the most beautiful girl that I had ever seen. She had a genuine sweetness and I could feel the Angels rejoicing but it seemed simply too good to be true.

Angelina – Wow, that message made my day special ☺ Thank you so much. I will recommend your book to many people. I'm so happy to connect with you ☺ <3

Robbie – It's always a pleasure to put a smile on someone's face. You have a very pretty smile too ☺ <3

There was a divine heart opening happening and I felt so good that I felt bad because I had promised to go and see the other girl in the morning. The next hour went by like it was a few minutes and I couldn't help sending love to her. Massive déjà vu's and a feeling of divine buoyancy engulfed me like I was floating on air. I had keep a hold of myself because I had been a parental figure to a girl who was only 4 years younger. I dismissed any romantic designs on her because of this. But that didn't stop the way I was feeling.

We continued chatting and it was the single most powerful messenger exchange that I have ever experienced. We were so polite and gentle, but underneath it was this massive energy that I knew must be contained. Because once it was unleashed, it would have been impossible to keep in check.

I went down to see the other girl and she decided to stop taking her meds. I told her I didn't think she should do that before consulting with her doctor. She insisted that she felt the heart opening of the Angels, declaring that she was cured. With what is diagnosed as bipolar with violent paranoid schizophrenia, it can be a very unpredictable and volatile situation.

I put myself to the side as much as possible and called in all the healing power of the Angels to help this lovely soul. I was, once again, in a situation where my compassion was overriding what was good for me. This continued for almost two months and I was led to understand her condition from a certain perspective. Part of it was her having a deep sensitivity to vibrations, different dimensions, and very acute but undeveloped telepathic medium-ship. The more open my heart became in compassion, the more balanced she seemed to be. But it was becoming obvious that I was not to be there as her lover. Spirits surrounded this girl that she couldn't make sense of.

I had entered the situation in a romantic capacity and while I could help her make sense of what was happening to a certain degree, the way she viewed me had an inflated savior aspect to it. And because she stressed that she had been hurt in the past, there was massive guilt projected preemptively in her dialogue that put me between a rock and a hard place. It was obvious because of this that we wouldn't be able to remain friends. It was all or nothing and she was sensing me drawing back already. Becoming verbally abusive and blaming me for her situation.

This was a major testing force for me because of my newfound expansion after the Shang Po initiation. It was calling me to impeccability and a deeper reliance on grace to be as sensitive to the situation as possible without losing myself in sacrifice or coercion from guilt as I had done many times before. And if I wasn't going to be there as a constant in the long term, I concluded that it would be better for both of us to quickly remove myself from the situation.

Angelina was still very much on my mind but I was struggling with it. Was this a mid-life crisis? In my readings, whenever I saw a mid-life crisis, the symbolism is usually the picture of a bald man with a sports car and a nineteen-year-old girlfriend. I didn't feel like my life had passed me by and I didn't have a wife and kids to be left in the wake of my disastrous choices. So what was I worried about? I was not prepared to do anything fully committed until the Metatron prophesy had been fulfilled. But I did start talking to my family and friends about maybe moving to Spain at some point.

As my tantric, kundalini raising powers had increased since the Shang Po initiation. I was sending out a lot of healing to different people. Of course, the one connection that was much more than just healing was Angelina. She had been directed towards fasting and surrendering to divine will since we said hello. As we connected one day telepathically and surrendered to the moment in detachment and acceptance of divine will. Surrendering my ego and without attachment to the outcome. I directed the most powerful energy that I had ever felt before to her. This resulted in her full Kundalini awakening and she was shaking for ten days. Not able to sleep and feeling the deepest divine power. Her life was forever changed and she now lives in complete reverence for God.

I went out with a Tantric masseuse next. This seemed like a good solution to my situation. But proved to be a challenging time as I loosened my romantic concepts and opened my mind to a different way of looking at relationships. This girl said that she wanted her idea of polyamory and had the philosophy that I was to love only her but could have sex with anyone that I wanted. This was in direct contradiction to what I believed was the ideal relationship. Even though I hadn't been able to fully commit a future to women. I had always been a serial monogamist. My belief was shaped by my parent's relationship where they had been completely faithful to each other till death. This was very stable for me as a child and something I felt instinctively was a good thing.

I opened my mind to this concept because I was still waiting for the lightning bolt visit from my Twin Flame. As time went on I deduced that this was a distancing mechanism this girl was using so she didn't have to connect too deeply. And when the time came for her to disconnect, the relationship had been diluted by unfaithfulness, albeit encouraged. But psychologically easing responsibility and so blame could be easily transferred. I could be wrong about this but it certainly fits with how it felt at the time. She was a very clever cookie in some ways as it seemed to all be worked out in advance. I don't think she believed that monogamy could end in anything other than pain. I understood this completely from my earlier pattern.

This time expanded my understanding of Tantra. And she said that I was the most powerful Daka (Tantric healer) that she had ever met. But my conclusion was that the strongest energy lovers cultivate can only be done in monogamy. Even though you have to work through your issues together for any kind of lasting authenticity. I have always sent tantric energies in a healing way to raise kundalini and remove blockages with my clients or chelas I had been presented with. But I saw this as a different issue because in a relationship, to be in the deepest tantric place. It has to be mind, body and spirit surrender.

Throughout this time I didn't exercise the 'Freedom' that I was being encouraged to indulge in physically. But Angelina did message me a few times. Each time was at either **11:11** am/pm, **2:22**, **4:44** etc. And I couldn't resist sending her energy, and definitely not just the healing kind. This proved to be more intense in the few times that we connected than the whole six-month relationship I was involved in.

At exactly six months, this girl informed me that we were finished and she had met someone else. Immediately after she hung up the phone it was **11:11**pm. Angelina messaged me and we exchanged pictures. Another divinely timed conversation. I met up with my new ex the next day so we could return house keys. And because the Edinburgh festival had started, we spent some time together and saw a show. She was telling me how happy she was and that the new guy was very special. I was pleased for her because any hurt that I could have experienced had been quickly canceled out by Angelina's messages. She found it hard to understand why I was being so nice to her and ramped up the praise for the other guy. I felt that this was another coping mechanism because breaking up with someone is never easy. And if she got me angry and jealous it would assuage her guilt and she could feel justified. But I wasn't affected at all. And during the show all I could think about was Angelina. As we were walking back, she asked to see the pictures I took of the Japanese drummers we had just watched. She flicked the pictures on my phone, came across the one that Angelina had sent me the night before and suddenly her attempts to make me jealous and angry backfired. She was in floods of tears and angry at me. I comforted her and calmed her down but it seemed to me that her bravado had been masking her true self and that spirit had organized the whole thing as a lesson for me.

The lesson I learned - **There is powerful potency in faithfulness when deeply understood and respected.**

True intimacy, when that is what both people want. Naturally excludes anyone else from the equation. If you approach relationships this way as a standard, you will come across your partner more quickly. Metatron told me that detachment and acceptance of divine will in this regard draws you towards your Twin Flame. In the readiness to become the very best version of yourself possible within this incarnation. I was learning more and more about myself and felt that all of these experiences were preparing me for her. Just as it had said in the Clarion Call.

"As you raise your vibration, your romantic life will change. If you are already with the partner that you are meant to be with, your relationship will get better, stronger. You will become wiser within your relationship. And if you are still looking for that partner, when you plug yourself into the matrix. If you properly open up your Merkaba. You will be introduced to your twin flame energy if they are on the Earth plane at the moment.

If they are in Spirit you will be introduced to them in a different way, and they will serve a different purpose to help you move forward in your spirituality. Instead, you will be united with a higher soul mate and your relationship will be one of joy, fun, passion and great sexual connection. Of great romance and of great intensity. And you will make a pair bonding that will last for the rest of your lives. Initially, this can be challenging. It is one of the most important things on your spiritual path and must be honored. In honoring yourself you will be honoring them. Give yourself and them space and time to assimilate the intensity of this relationship that is coming into your being. As your vibration raises and intensifies, so will theirs. And your potential will be multiplied. For a light-worker is mighty and powerful. But a light-worker connected to a higher soul mate or twin flame energy can be ten times more powerful when you are operating from your higher chakras and allowing Spirit to flow through you.

Allowing my voltage to flow through you and purifying yourselves, you can reach a higher point of potential. Through sacred sex, sacred communion, sacred eating, joining your consciousness and ascending together. And spreading this love throughout humanity. You will enjoy yourself much better when you understand this. Give yourself over to your higher self and emancipate yourself from your vessel. Be brave enough to push your light forward." – Metatron, this is the Clarion Call.

I felt like I was ready for this. But I had learned so much over the last few years that I just had to trust that each different part of my own personal jigsaw was falling into place. I was chatting with many women, waiting on her coming to Scotland. It felt a little like an old traditionally sexist role reversal. Instead of being the one waiting for my knight in shining armor. I was waiting for my lady in a beautiful white dress to ride in on her unicorn. I couldn't give any instruction about the conditions of how it was to happen to anyone, so all I could do was wait and trust.

The year that Angelina finally came to Scotland, I was asked to do another long fast and bring down the next Metatron book. This was to be a forty day fast and would introduce the 'Metatron tradition' of healing. It was a short workbook and a very pure endeavor. I was made aware that everything that had happened in the previous year was important for this work as it was vital to have a raised kundalini for the flow of divine healing to be infused deeply into the words. This book introduced energetic **Downloads** and **Upgrades**, which were very overwhelming and left me with a heightened sense of grace. I was being upgraded myself as I continued with the channelings and what I had been through up till now started to make great sense.

"This next download is to open up and awaken your divine Kundalini, your divine sexuality. This will take away the shame, the negativity and all detrimental effects that have been put upon your consciousness through society, through religion, through your familial understanding. This will help clear your filter system and bring you into your divine God/Goddess selves so that you may embrace your sexuality and that your kundalini will rise through your base chakra up to your crown chakra. And you may feel the flow of energy and not waste it in disrespect or negativity and will help you honor this for yourself and for all others that you come into contact with in a sexual way.

Your sexuality is a gift from the Universe. It is a wonderful and powerful healing tool when understood correctly, to help Mankind free themselves from the bondage that they have been under for millennia. All the abuse that has happened, all the pain that has been inflicted, has been because as a species you have manipulated and misled each other to the belief that your sexual connections are wrong, unholy, and sinful.

Even believing that sin is what created you in the physical. This is not the truth dear ones, you are sexual beings and once you embrace this within your vessels, no matter what your orientation is, once you embrace yourself, you will help the world be more at ease with themselves. And all the pain that has come out of these negative concepts will be released.

As you begin to understand the power of your sexual energy as it flows through your body, instead of merely understanding it from a physical perspective of genital excitement. When you understand and honor this, your Kundalini will be free to flow and your power to heal others, to free others, to awaken others and to embody the bliss of your own sexuality will multiply your powers of healing." - Metatron, this is the Healing Book.

I was once again having the same feelings that I had experienced on my 16th birthday. Many souls seemed to be joining together in meditation and raising the vibration of the planet. I was reminded of the experiment that a group of meditators did in Washington DC in 1993 where they claimed they could reduce the crime rate by 20%. This was ridiculed by the local police chief who stated that the only way this could happen would be under 20 inches of snow. They did the study in the summer and it was just getting hotter and hotter, which usually resulted in more crime rather than less and yet the final results showed that the overall drop in HRA crime (Homicide, rape and aggravated assaults) was 23.3%. Which continued throughout the two-month experiment. The chances of this happening randomly was less than 2 in 1 billion. It made sense why I was feeling this and remembering this study as I continued with the healing books next download.

"This next download is for you to help the leaders of the World let go of their egos and be in their integrity. Seeing them all with an immaculate conception so that they may break the shackles of outside economic interests and hold their offices in pure integrity. Wherever you are

geographically in the World this is best directed to your closest leader first and then at all leaders so that there will be harmony.

You do not have to be involved in individual issues politically, however, you will be led by your passion to what it is you are here to fulfill. Always be ready and open to accept that a divine solution will be in your better interest more than one you feel led by your ego to make a stand for. For all is not always as it seems. There is an organization that is going on, on the Earth plane right now. Do not resist anything for at this point in your vibration it is most important to see the bigger picture and to allow the Angelic influences to do their work. As Masters you are individually responsible for the raising of the vibration and for being in bliss and in peace which will result in your leaders being given the support to straighten their mental bodies in such a way that they facilitate the transition of this Earth from ego led, power based decision making which is influenced by separate economic interests to that of a pure, transparent and divinely acceptable way of being governed." – Metatron, this is the Healing Book.

This was very exciting when I realized the implications of this study, connected with this download. When there are enough people who commit to this as a standard and use this gift to help support those imbued with the power to make change on a bureaucratic level. The World will transform very rapidly indeed.

I was thinking about my own physical healing and how I had instinctively stopped using the drugs I had been given. Why did I have such a conviction that this was the right thing to do? The next part of the book discussed this very thing.

"You are more powerful than you have been led to believe and your ability to heal is much stronger than you have been led to believe also. Even many of your

physicians do not understand your healing power as they are being trained to deal with your symptoms instead of the root cause of your problems. The understanding of medicine will come on leaps and bounds the more of you that awaken and the more that vibrational energy and healing are integrated into your medicinal paradigms.

Do not misunderstand us – the majority of doctors who take your Hippocratic oath are very eager to heal and to help. But the majority of that system in its current paradigm is based upon the selling of drugs instead of the understanding of wellbeing." - Metatron, this is the Healing Book.

Could this really be the truth? Is the majority of healthcare based on the selling of drugs? What proof was there of this and how could this have become the norm? I synchronistically came across an article right then in sciencebasedmedicine.org by Harriet Hall MD called 'Most patients get no benefit from most drugs' which talks about the **NNT**. The numbers needed to treat for one person to benefit. The numbers are rarely discussed in the mainstream. Many treatments have no evidence of benefit at all! That doesn't stop the drugs being prescribed though. Doctors know this. So for the pharmaceutical industry that makes over a trillion dollars a year in profits, most of their products don't benefit most of their customers. This isn't a sensationalist statement. These are medical statistics. In ancient China, the doctor didn't get paid if their patient was unwell. It was seen as unethical to accept money for a service that wasn't effective. Seems like ancient wisdom took care of us much better in many ways than our modern 'civilization'.

The big problem is that many medicines are amazing, life-saving and vital to healing. This is a stranglehold position that is taken advantage of by the business side of the equation.

These numbers are debated by different, equally qualified people in the medical profession. But the numbers are very important for us to have an informed opinion about what we are taking into our precious bodies. Especially if the odds are low in efficacy and high in side effects. The other number is the **NNH**, the numbers needed to harm. When we can statistically say that prescription drugs are sometimes quoted as being the 4th biggest cause of death in the whole world. Surely we need to scrutinize the system. We trust our doctors. They have trained for years to be able to prescribe these medicines and of course we should have a degree of trust if we are to have any peace of mind. And yet doctors with the same degrees hold different opinions as to what works and what doesn't. So how can we make an informed choice without having all of the information before us?

It's important to be able to see objectively without having the dangerous attitude of having a little information and the bravado to talk expertly. The Dunning-Kreuger effect is a cognitive bias that states that the less you know, the less you can tell how little you know. Conversely, the opposite is true of those scientifically and medically trained and knowledgeable in their field. Though having a greater understanding, they have a greater awareness of how little they know. This is why it is important for dialogue to be with respect and humility from both standpoints with all subjects.

Looking at the statistics is just as important as looking at the studies, where the studies were funded, and who stands to gain from a positive outcome of any drug trial or endorsing medical opinion. With so many kickbacks for the medical profession, Is your doctor's priority your health or their wallet.

Just now, as I am writing this, I came across a brilliant documentary called 'What the health'. This featured the doctor whose books helped convince me, along with Metatron, that it was possible to reverse diabetes. Dr Neal Barnard MD. The studies and trials he is involved in, which are funded without any financial profit bias, show overwhelmingly that a plant-based diet is the best way to treat and can even cure a lot of these diseases. However, in this documentary, it reveals that the very institutions that are meant to help us by recommending the proper diet and steps to take to help or even cure diabetes, cancer, heart disease etc. Are actually sponsored by the makers of products that give us those diseases in the first place. This documentary illustrates that meat and dairy producers and many pharmaceutical companies work in tandem with each other to keep us fed with carcinogenic and chemical laden food which ultimately requires us to have pharmaceutical treatment according to their model. A plant-based diet can be curing, revitalizing, and life-affirming. Leaving less need for medical treatment and, simply put, healthier people… Not much money in that though!

"Giving up animal products not only heals your vessel and helps you become a more effective healer, but it helps the world and helps break down the systems that are in place right now that are forcing a fear vibration over the whole of humanity. Not only this but in giving up animal products you will be helping the world towards economic freedom. This is the most important thing as divine healers that you will actively do to heal yourself, to heal others and to heal the planet, Do not take this point lightly for the majority of things that need to be healed will be healed by this simple act once it is embraced by the whole of humanity. This is where your species are heading as you understand the nature of disease and you make the commitment to really heal the world, to really heal others and to really heal yourself. This is not a point that can be ignored. As you begin to embrace a plant based diet your vibration will raise rapidly." - Metatron, this is the Healing Book.

Modern medicine is magnificent in many ways. And we are much better off because of the great advances that have been made with it. But if we are, in the main, addressing what goes wrong as a result of dangerously damaging fundamentals in our fuelling and habits. We will always be spending our energy taking the water out of the boat. Instead of filling in the holes that are causing the leak in the first place. And if we are not even prepared to look at these things objectively with proper scrutiny. Then who do we have to blame but ourselves?

Then God said, "I give you every seed bearing plant on the face of the whole Earth and every tree that has fruit with seed in it. They will be yours for food." - Genesis 1:29

Serendipity

I finished the book in the forty days and the time was drawing near to midsummer. I could feel something big getting ready to happen and was detaching as much as possible. I didn't know what it was, but there was magic in the air. Angelina told me later that although she was initially convinced that we were meant to be together, she had finally given up on the idea because of my lack of action and apparent lack of romantic interest. I too had given up on any specific person, even though Angelina had always been the best case scenario. I was contemplating becoming a celibate tantric healer, concentrating solely on my divine channeling and work for God. We had both authentically given up on the idea of a relationship at the same time. This was when the magic happened.

Angelina was unexpectedly invited to go on a trip to Iona. The holy isle in Scotland. With a group of spiritual seekers. She initially turned it down because of not being very happy with me and didn't want to seem like she was chasing me and was content to concentrate on her yoga and meditation anyway. But her late Fathers old friend Richard was very persistent and led by the holy spirit to ask her again and again. Everything was paid for and the ticket to Scotland was delivered to her door. Everything had fallen into place and so, after consulting with the Angels, she decided to come to Scotland.

The time finally came and I found out she was going to be in Scotland shortly before midsummer. Her group had completed their time in Iona. So she was free to do her own thing. We agreed to meet in the Salutation hotel, in Kinross. She asked if we should have a wee drink together but after doing a channeling I said that I was being told to keep a clear head. I guess there was a wee bit of mischievous energy mixed with nerves in the air because I bought a lager when I arrived. I then searched upstairs in the hotel where there was a pool table and the most stunning girl I had ever clapped eyes on in my life. Sitting with her own lager. She was wearing a little black dress with her hair in a ponytail and we flashed the biggest smiles at each other.

The first hour was the most surreal mix of potent, powerful, electric eye gazing and soul speak. The time went by very quickly as our souls took over and we had what I can only describe as a soul merge experience. While sitting across from each other. Completely at ease. Like we had always been together. Very powerfully sending lightning bolts of energy through each other. Like the Gods of Tantra had plugged us into the main frame of divine, sensual expansion. After some time I was gripped by a deep urge to kiss her and I leaned over the table. Slowly we physically connected for the first time. It was the most romantic moment I had ever experienced and what must have been only a few seconds, seemed like an eternity, as our lips touched. It felt more like a reconnection than a first connection. We were in an almost trance-like state and as we came away from each other. Our eyes opened and lit up in the divine realization of our oneness. The rest of the night was spent going for walks by Loch Leven and popping into different pubs as we got to know each other. We fell asleep, fully clothed, in each other's arms. It was the best night of my life.

Angelina asked me to channel for the first time in front of her in the morning and was so moved that she was brought to tears. The guides were very pleased with our progress. They suggested we do a ten-day juice fast together, starting in a few days. I left the hotel and was floating on air as I went back to my house.

An Impromptu marriage

After Angelina had been with me for a few days, I thought it would be a nice gesture to get her a reading from a local medium that I really respected who had recently returned to the area. Years ago she was the one who channeled the message that told me of the two books by Metatron I would channel that would help with the coming ascension of humanity. This was ten years later and the first time I'd seen her since then. Sure enough, I had recently channeled the second book from Metatron that she had mentioned. We went through to Kirkcaldy, the town where her shop is, and she was there, having tea when we arrived.

"Oh, my, Saraswati!" she proclaimed, upon seeing Angelina. I had thought maybe she could give Angelina an Ascended Masters or Angel reading and I asked about it, but Marie-Louise had different ideas. She suggested a couple reading that she could do the following week. We were delighted, as neither of us had had a couple reading before.

The day came for our reading and we dressed up as if it was a really special occasion. There was excitement in the air and when we arrived, Marie-Louise said that she had been up since 3 am because of our union and the intense energies that she was being directed with. She suggested that as well as the channeled message, that she could perhaps do a cleansing and seated chair healing on us both as part of the ceremony, but that she would just go with the divine flow and do what she was directed to do as most of the time would be spent with her in trance. We were very happy to go with the flow of the Holy Spirit too.

Marie-Louise asked us to sit on either side of her and hold each other's hands, as well as hers, forming a triangle and she surrendered into a deep trance state. The energies were very powerful as the Masters spoke through her and the room was filled with divine light. Instead of a prophetic message about the strengths and weaknesses of our connection and what we should look out for and our horoscopes etc, the energy was very sacred and definite about what was about to happen. As the Masters spoke, the stage was set for something that neither of us had expected.

We were inspired to intuitively say sacred and Holy words to each other that felt much deeper and more profound than a traditional marriage ceremony. The words were very beautiful and we were in tears as time went on and the Holy healing and cleansing took place. As the channeling continued, the Masters mentioned this being the Hieros Gamos ceremony that we have participated in together, in many lifetimes before. And it was the perfect time for our spirits to begin the deep journey together in this lifetime. We left the ceremony feeling lighter than air and a little dazed as it felt like we had just got married after having physically known each other for only a week. But even though they were very powerful words we had professed to each other, it didn't feel forced or too soon. It felt like we had always been a couple and we were just coming back together again.

We took a bus through to Edinburgh to celebrate. As we sat bathing in each other's aura, a ladybird landed on my hand and kept flying back and forth between the seats around us. Angelina said that the ladybird was the sign of her Dad, who had passed away three years previously and it was like he was there, blessing the divine union. It was a wonderful sign and an unexpectedly beautiful day. I joked with Angelina that I had set this all up as a romantic gesture. But the truth was that I had no idea that this was going to happen, and couldn't have been happier.

I mentioned to Sally a few days later what had happened and told her that the name of the ceremony was the Hieros Gamos. She was surprised and excited and said: "Did you know that unlike marriage, you can only do that ceremony once in a lifetime?!"

I had no idea and did some research on the Hieros Gamos. Carl Gustav Jung, the chap that first explained synchronicity, the concept that seemingly unrelated events coinciding are not really coincidences but have a deeper meaning, studied the Hieros Gamos. He discovered that the main purpose of the ceremony was the reuniting of two people in a sacred marriage that was not just for anyone. This ceremony was energetically recognizing the two halves of the single soul that was synchronistically brought together by divine will, specifically for the time of ascension of a species. This ceremony was specifically for Twin Flames! This made perfect sense with the channeling that Metatron had given me almost ten years earlier. It all felt so familiar and complete. This ceremony, to me, was much more important than the one I had done officially in legally marrying someone else, and yet we had just met. I am definitely an old romantic.

In the beginning too

From an early age, Angelina was aware of different dimensions also. She was very sensitive and due to distressing early experiences was in an almost constant state of alert and developed severe anxiety, panic attacks, and O.C.D. Her early life, growing up in Malta, had a feeling of island safety and the security of familiarity with her childhood friends. At age ten she moved away to Hungary, then England and in both she was in strict religious schools where they believed in Hell and punishment, coinciding with my parent's beliefs. The threat of Hellfire was ever present but Angelina knew there was something different out there. The next move was to sunny Spain at age fourteen. She still continued to be in private education at first but the harsh energies were too much and she finally insisted that she went to public school. In class, they left her alone to read for the first year as she didn't know Spanish yet and in this time, because she didn't feel as much pressure, she was able to relax and was allowed to bring in her own books. Reading texts like 'Awakening intuition' by Mona Lisa Schulz and 'Cosmic ordering' by Barbel Mohr, she felt inspired and great beauty would flow into her experience.

The second year, however, things took a different turn. She was bullied, and after her parents split up, she experienced grooming from a middle aged sexual predator. Nobody believed her about it and over the next few years, he gradually took her innocence. At 17 he took her away to be a tantric Masseuse in Germany for a year. She was on the Interpol lost persons list but finally escaped his brainwashing and manipulation when she had a really sore tummy and wanted to see a Doctor. He told her that no treatment was needed, but she managed to contact her Mum and Dad and they took her to the hospital. The Doctor rushed her straight in because she had an abnormal pregnancy with such terrible complications that could have killed her had it not been caught in time. Feeling betrayed, confused and dishonored, she eventually fell into cyclical drinking habits. Not able to connect to an intimate relationship unless intoxicated. Her late teens were a haze of dysfunction and despair. This mirrored a lot of my own experience.

Angelina's Dad, her best friend, and greatest confidant passed away from what the doctors called 'The most aggressive form of cancer they had ever seen' at the age of 54. This was the hardest time in her life and was the catalyst for her spiritual seeking. She found her divine center while living alone, finally in her own aura for two years. An Angel course would help change her life towards a consciously spiritual existence. Doing yoga, praying and meditating. She finally felt herself amongst a community of people who genuinely understood her path, even if most of them were online. Her Kundalini awakening was the most powerful change and after her ten days of shaking, her habits became more regulated and she never again felt the urge to overeat or drink heavily.

We did the juice fast together and got used to being in each other's Auras at last. It was a very intense few weeks. Our prayer, meditation, and divine work had started together and everything flowed. The time went by very quickly. Before she left, Angelina asked me to come and live with her in Spain. I had been in the council house in Scotland for over ten years and had always felt it was important that I stay there and keep it on. I had even contemplated buying it as I would get a great deal for having rented for so long, and the 'right to buy' still applied. But as soon as Angelina arrived I was ready to pack up and leave. Our mission had already begun together and I was eager to finally get moving.

I spent the next six weeks selling most of my possessions and giving up my house. Angelina's Mum messaged me and officially invited me to come to stay. I was downsizing and getting ready for whatever the Universe had in store for me. After almost ten years of waiting since Metatrons channeling, she had finally arrived and I was diving in head first.

Then it hit me like a ton of bricks. What was I doing? I had only known this woman in the flesh for less than two weeks. I was leaving the safety and security of the familiar. My family, friends, and surroundings. Letting go of all of my possessions and trusting that I was making the right move. Did I doubt our connection? Not for a second. Did I trust in God? Completely. So what was this moment and how would it define my future. It was how I would imagine it feels at the top of a bungee platform or on a parachute jump. Just before you pass the point of no return. I had waited on this for a long time and the actual experience had surpassed all of my expectations. It felt like I had just won the lottery. I could see my potential and hers being fulfilled more completely than with any other circumstance. And above all, I could feel, more than at any other time, that this was divinely orchestrated. And I would be a fool to not jump at this opportunity. But once again it seemed too good to be true and this trepidation welded me to the spot. Pondering the ramifications of my actions in many different situations that I had been in before where I had jumped in feet first. I suddenly realized the biggest difference. This was what I wanted. Wholly and completely. I wasn't being coerced, manipulated or guilted into it. And at that moment the trepidation turned back into excitement and joy about the future. No matter what form it would take. God was in charge and I was completely on board. Floating on the certainty of faith and convinced that there was a great adventure ahead.

"The bold adventurer succeeds the best." – Ovid

I arrived in Spain and we spent five weeks at Angelina's Mums villa in Elviria. We soon got our own wee flat not too far away, so we could properly start our life together in privacy.

It had not been that long since I channeled the healing book and I was still assimilating the energies. The upgrades and downloads were having a profound impact on my waking consciousness. I was opening to concepts of other life forms being a reality. Not just multi-dimensional, but physical and imminently feeling their presence. The Kundalini download was affecting us both and our divine light was shining the more and more we were in each other's Auras and the deeper the energy of it was accepted.

"There is an excitement surrounding this download such as you have never experienced before opening your kundalini. And this flow awakens you to the new humanity of love, trust, and divine sexuality. With this download, we increase the power. This download is deeply connected to your emotional body. This will take down all the barriers and will allow you to be in a flow state. Breathe deeply and embrace what is going on in your vessel just now." – Metatron, this is the Healing book.

This energy was bringing us face to face with the pain that we had both been through in this lifetime. Trust issues and abuses from the past were being highlighted from our shadow sides to be cleared. The deeper the tenderness and more intense the Tantric connection, the more vulnerable we became and we were shown what needed to be healed within us. I was healing her and she was healing me of things I didn't even know I needed healing from.

"This healing book is for your healing personally. For you healing others in their four-body system and also for healing the World" – Metatron, this is the Healing book.

I had been blessed since starting this journey all those years ago. And the more people that contacted me to thank me for channeling the books, the more I felt validated and motivated. Many people told me that the books had completely changed their lives and I could feel the shift happening on Earth very intensely.

"You are creating new paradigms on this Earth. Clearing the complications of negative dogma and doctrine from the past. Changing the consciousness of the World. The balance of light has already tipped in the favor of the new opening consciousness. In your linear understanding of time, this happened at the Winter solstice in 2012. It is a subtle change but the balance has been tipped towards an opening, awakening, truthful understanding with Humanities curiosity and acceptance. Feeling that good things are ahead for your species." – Metatron, this is the Healing book.

After six months we moved again, this time to a mountain top house in Calahonda. A time of intense exercise, Yoga and a new fast that I had been asked to do. So that I could channel the next in the series of ascension books. I started the fast and was walking up and down the mountain side twice a day. We were literally feeling the effects of the downloads happening as described.

"As you assimilate these Galactic energies your whole body will start to tingle. Your whole body will start to vibrate with excitement at the higher resonance; the

higher vibration. And you will begin to see things changing in your own lives, the lives of those around you and the vibration of the World in general" – Metatron, this is the Healing book.

It came to day twenty of the fast and I started the new books. I was introduced to a character called Bashanthi Mayawar. This translates to 'body of peace that helps with the war of illusion'. This being was a perfect mix of male and female and did not specify their gender. I could feel great benevolence with them and had a feeling like I was a school-kid on their first day at high school being shown around by an older kid. This made perfect sense with one of the first channelings.

"As newbie's here you may feel very overwhelmed as you did at the beginning of your school days. But very soon you understood the routine of this new world of schooling. And you came to an understanding of your place within this system. Unlike your Human schools, the hierarchical system does not wish to take any energy from you, ridicule you or self-aggrandize. All new members have great wisdom in their innocence and we honor this wisdom." - The Galactic Council.

It was an important point. Even talking about extra terrestrials in any way other than in a fictional sense usually invokes ridicule and derision. Why is this? What is there to be scared of? And why doesn't it make perfect sense that if we are being observed by advanced races that they would want to communicate with us telepathically first before shocking us by landing ships en masse. It has only been a decade since we first had iPhones, and that technology has changed the world as we know it. What was science fiction when I was a kid is now an everyday reality. The existence of humans is a tiny blip, time-wise, from what we know about the time life has had to evolve on this planet. That's just the physical Universe. Other dimensions give us the concept of an infinite timeline. So if there are much older species that invented their iPhone equivalent millions or even billions of years ago, it seems very plausible that they could have the technology for them to stay undetected while we play catch-up.

"Are we alone? Probably not, unless you are inexcusably egocentric" – Neil deGrasse Tyson

I was being asked to powerfully expand myself with exercise before each channeling. This hadn't happened before. Sometimes I would start a channeling and they would ask me to do 100 sit-ups and 100 press-ups before continuing. This was affecting my system in such a positive way that the bliss during each channeling was on a whole new level. I knew that things had been stepped up and I had been experimenting with bi-locating in my Merkaba during meditation for some time. Joining my NYC group in Central Park and helping different people raise their energies. But I didn't expect the next part to be quite so intense. Usually, in a channeling, the consciousness that I allow to use my system is in that position during the whole time. There is usually a flow and they don't tend to stutter. But the next channeling was something that I had not experienced before.

"There are many different beings that wish to contribute to this book. We had to be very discerning so you are not overwhelmed. The channel chosen that is downloading this right now is seeing for the first time the collection of beings on the Galactic Council in Orion. As this is all being recorded we shall detach our vibration for a few minutes in order to let Robbie explain what it is that he is seeing.

"Thank you Bashanthi (laughs nervously) it is actually quite beautiful. There is a, what looks like a... ballroom, massive big place. It looks like something out of Star Wars and there's... lots of... different beings with different shaped heads that are em, it looks (Laughs) very happy... to see me... laughs.. em...(Coughs)... it's emm... quite overwhelming... but I can feel the energy of benevolence... err with these people, beings, em... ahh... I erm... I don't quite know what the etiquette is here... (Laughs) this has never happened to me in a channeling before...emmm... its nice to meet you... there's a chap that looks like a big fish (Laughs) but that has legs... and

em... well they all have legs but there's a chap hovering that doesn't have legs em that's wearing a top hat... And there's a purple being, very tall, looks like the singing wifey from the fifth element... the place is really big, it's massive it's like... Like the size of a football stadium and there's a big glass dome at the top and I can see... through there it looks like the em... there's a planet that looks really really big and looks really green and looks like Earth looks but not like Earth like the same similar colours to Earth but not like it's the shapes of the land masses are different... there's just an overwhelming feeling of benevolence... (laughs)... I feel drunk, I don't even drink (Laughs)... and I feel like I'm standing in this place... I know I'm in my office but I feel like I'm standing in this place and they are all surrounding me like being very inquisitive and emm... They are looking very humble but also there's a chap with a big trunk, like an Elephant trunk (Laughs) and there is aaaa... chap that looks like a Tiger... like all these different people, they are like people, not like ... I don't want to be disrespectful but they look like animals but they don't look wild, they look like they are evolved em (Laughs) ... I'm starting to... its like I'm losing the vision now... it's like I felt like I was standing in the place but I feel like it's been taken back now so erm... Thank you for that experience Bashanthi... That was really... very cool (Laughs)... I can't stop laughing now (laughs) ... I feel like I'm full of cosmic energy... thank you for that. That was... very powerful!" – The Galactic Council.

The cosmic waves were so potent that I was glowing for the coming days. It also reinforced my recognition of the importance of why they would initiate contact on a telepathic level first with mankind. I was used to thinking about these concepts on a real level. But actually feeling face to face with different intelligent species was truly overwhelming. Exciting and fun too though, and, once again, a whole new worldview opened up in me thereafter.

Our twin flame bond was magnifying everything. And all of the challenges that we had both faced were now doubling in intensity. Mixed with the bliss of our passion were the demons of our dark side. My masculine side was growing and her feminine side too. Twin flames are not always male/female but the yin/yang within them always comes into balance because of the energy of a single shared soul. Before it can balance it has to be highlighted. And any abuse in the way we have been conditioned, intentionally or not, is given center stage to be healed before you can fully step into your power. And the more cosmic energy that you embody or are surrounded with, speeds up this process.

You will inevitably be blamed, or feel you are being blamed for past abuses. With the same token, your twin flame will feel the same. Not because either of you is to blame. But because the love, passion, and intensity open you and them up to the feeling of complete trust on a soul level. This sounds counter-intuitive but that safety allows for the issues to surface. Even if you thought you had dealt with all of your issues and are generally in bliss. This divine love will show you what you need to work on. This is true to a certain extent of all loving relationships when you feel safe. But the twin flame connection is about more than just romance, security and comfort. It is a training ground for complete mastery and stepping into the best version of yourself. So that you can embody not only passionate couple love but divine Avataric unconditional love. What you focus on is the most important thing together.

"Your Tantric freedom is ready to arrive and the affect you will have on your partner will be immense when you are in your zero point. Every touch will become an ecstasy; every thought will be a flowering of passion. You are moving into a new realm of understanding of the effect your four-body system can have on each other. For when you come together with your Twin Flame you form a golden bubble of love together that no other can penetrate. And you penetrate each other deeply, mentally, emotionally, physically and spiritually, your souls connecting as one. You will have a deep connection,

from your base chakra to your crown chakra, with your heart chakras on fire, and the profound safety and transcendence of the golden bubble that you have together. Initially, you will be in the golden bubble together as two halves in the whole. But then you will merge into each other and the golden bubble will be one.

This is a deeply profound experience and when you are in this sacred place with your Twin Flame it is not just your sexuality that will open up. Every part of you will flower. Your mental bodies will be brought into alignment. You will recognize the role you have within the male-female connection no matter your orientation. You will come into balance with your own male-female connection in your Merkaba within yourself. And you will link together your joint Merkaba as two halves of the same soul. And you will transcend all dimensions. Your emotional body coming to balance and being in the center place together will bring you into the peace that passes understanding. And will expand your heart chakra more than you thought possible. For in this place you are Mother, Father God. You are creator and creatrix of the universe. Shiva and Shakti, hardness and softness, passionate transcendence, awakened power that will transform you. All aspects of your being for you will be a catalyst for each others growth.

If you focus on the zero point, if you focus on God, if you focus on the oneness, whichever way you quantify the all that is. If you focus on this instead of each other, you will ascend and you will be brought into your full potential. And you will achieve things you never thought possible. Your lovemaking will take your breath away. Your physical vessels will improve in health, in stamina, in power, in fitness, and in sensitivity. And your spiritual bodies will join together as one flame. And when you make your focus God, your mission will become apparent.

You will work together as a team and you will have an unbreakable bond. Your telepathy will be great, your trust will be complete, and your passion will be beyond words. All that can hold you down in any mental thought form will be dissolved and cut away. You will transcend all things together.

If you focus on each other, and your ego structures, the opposite of this will happen. And you will pull into a negative spiral. Recognize that you can always turn this around by focusing on God, by focusing on the oneness and by detaching from the importance of your relationship and attaching onto the importance of God, you will be brought together and in this purification, you will transcend all boundaries. There will be nothing that you will not be able to accomplish together.

This is the most holy of relationships and it is always for a divine purpose that you are being brought together. The only way to be truly with your Twin Flame is to focus only on God, Divinity, the oneness, your Merkaba, and your transcendence. If you do this all things will be added unto you." - The Galactic Council.

We were going through the stages of focusing on each other and then focusing on God. Each time our focus was on each other we were given an ego lesson. Where something was brought up to be cleared. Even though I had dealt with a lot of my weight issues, I was still yo-yoing in between cleanses. Much less than before but I had not fully mastered it yet. And was going through different subtle points of control drama to justify my bad habits. The mirror of this for Angelina was alcohol and the same control dramas were apparent. Our seminal conditioning was being magnified and each time we went through a purging and out of control point, we ended up bringing ourselves back to balance using Ho'oponpono together. Prayer and meditation were vital in our transformation.

Ho'oponopono – A prayer for forgiveness and transformation through love. It begins with remorse for actions or words spoken. In starting this way, no matter the situation, it opens an energy of humility, which helps dissolve the ego and opens the flow of connection and light once again. Our version of this prayer together is – **"I'm sorry, please forgive me, thank you, I love you, all is well, all karma is clear, we are one."** This is to level or zero point all transgressions personally. For the other person and in the wider context, the whole world. We are all creating this reality together so the more we understand our part in the creation of it, the quicker we shall take responsibility for the way our energy impacts the whole.

Creating a diversion is what the ego is master at doing. Whenever love threatens to unveil the illusion. It clings to its reality in any way possible to dramatize any part of the current set up. What we think we are, or identify ourselves with, in our perceived incomplete form. Is highlighted to disempower us so that we submit to the illusion. Any thoughts of our own lack are preyed upon and used mercilessly to reaffirm the position of the ego. Past hurts are highlighted and the memory of them used like a surgeons scalpel the closer true love threatens to unveil and heal the wound previously inflicted. The closer we get to the truth of ourselves, the tougher the testing force of our ego separation becomes. Control dramas are the most obvious way we act as we embody a position of opposition from intimidating, interrogating, being aloof or adopting a poor me stance as was illustrated in 'The Celestine Prophecy'. These things are not always just a struggle to compete for energy. They are also ways to divert attention from the truth of our divinity that is waiting patiently for us to discover.

We were being put into situations that tested our commitment to being in the flow on a continuous basis. The deeper the love, the stronger the testing force seemed. The greater mastery you embody, the subtler and more disguised the testing force is also. This journey is of form and separation. And the task of our spiritual evolution is to bring the formless to form and weed out all obstacles to our divinity.

"The purer you become, the closer to the Godhead you approach, the stronger is the testing. Whatever needs to be worked out within your personal aura and your ego, within your mental, emotional, physical and spiritual bodies will be the focus of this testing. It will be very personal to you. The closer you are to the summit, the more surreal will seem the circumstance. Patience is the key to overcoming this" - The Galactic Council.

Purity in this context isn't a hellfire judgment thing. This purity just means the degree that you have freed yourself from any belief system that is clouding the connection to your divine source.

Angelina had a dream of her dog Snowy passing away soon. We had some confirmation in a channeling that it would be a good idea to go to be with her for her last months. So we packed our bags and set off for Hungary to live with Mama, Angelina's elderly Granny until we got our own flat in Budapest. I was informed that I would not be able to get a flat until I had completed the Galactic Council books. So I continued the Channelings once we arrived. We did look for a flat but could not secure one at all. Being with Mama was a lovely experience but had its testing points. She has dementia and such deep love that she is a powerhouse of energy, even though she has a tiny frame. She talked constantly to me in Hungarian and because I was good at reading her wishes and desires from her energy, she believed that I understood her. Memory problems can make for a very repetitious experience and when leaving the stove on full and not allowing the dogs to go out and do their business etc, it can bring the stress of heightened alert. Angelina was tested to the max with her O.C.D and anxiety at a high level. Old family testing forces were at play for her and I had to mediate the energy and try to help master things for us all while fasting and absorbing all of the cosmic energies of the Galactic Channelings.

"The Christ heart is blossoming on earth right now. The many masters are waking up. As you are reading this book you are moving into your mastery and the recognition that you can do something about the state of affairs on the Earth plane right now. The greatest gift you

can give the world is always your own enlightenment, always your own open Merkaba, always your own joy and always your own peace. **For the state of any world is always a reflection of the consciousness of its people.** So there is never judgment of any species that are ready to take the next leap in their evolution. The polarity always deepens before the breakthrough of mass consciousness change. So in understanding this you have the choice to dive deep into the illusion or to free yourself and create your own illusion. The platform for your illusion changes as your vibration rises. Therefore the most important thing is that you open your Merkaba. That you open yourselves in meditation and that you recognize the reality that you have helped create in this lifetime. The more you see things as they really are rather than as your filter system would have you believe they are. With the many different influences that have been in your consciousness. The easier it will be to transition to the state of bliss, continual bliss, divine bliss. You have all the tools you ever need with an open Merkaba and we encourage you to work towards the ring pass not, as we are eager to work with you physically in the galactic council as well as telepathically." - The Galactic Council.

When they talk about the Christ heart it means the unconditional love from your heart chakra. It is just as correct to say Krishna heart or Buddha heart, or whatever way you understand divinity from your own personal perspective.

The Ring pass what?

The most common question I get asked about the Clarion Call is "What exactly is the ring pass not?" The ring pass not is a failsafe device in your consciousness. It's like a valve of sorts that prevents you from being able to access energy and abilities that you would not be able to handle before you are ready. Because your higher consciousness/God/Spirit, whatever you want to call it. Knows everything about you much better than your waking mind does. It will only take off the stabilizers when it knows for sure that you can ride safely. There are many levels of this happening on your individual journey as well as collectively. One of these points is about the existence of other intelligent life forms visiting Earth.

The deeper I went into the cleanse and the channelings, the more profound became the messages. The ring pass not had not been focused on so much since the Clarion call had been channeled but then suddenly it was mentioned again as far as the collective experience that we have created together is concerned with regards to Palestine in the middle east.

"This is a great point of you coming to the understanding of what is needed to pass the ring pass not. What has been used as a weapon of misinformation to mislead the World by misusing the words Anti-Semitic in order to manipulate the World is a point that needs to be pondered. And the fear of this misuse and leverage of guilt upon the World to further the aims and ends of those who would enslave the World through misuse of the Holy name and misrepresentation of that which must remain Holy, is now coming to an end. With the beings of light that will only stand for the truth. The truth of this manipulation will set you free dear ones. This situation will come to an

end. For the kingdom of God is within all beings and those who have used the holy name for maniacal and despotic aims shall understand what karmic retribution is as the World comes together in unity. The brotherhood of man is accepted, and the kingdom of God is finally established on the Earth. Righteousness rather than self-righteousness will prevail and your World will come to peace." – The Galactic Council.

It seemed like a very important statement and one that I needed to look at more closely. The horrendous atrocities of the second world war are definitely not something that we want to ever have repeated. Genocide anywhere will not be possible in a truly enlightened global society. Because the level of sensitivity will be such that all beings will feel the effects on a deeper empathic level. So the only real way to prevent these things happening in the long term is to raise consciousness. This affects things in two significant ways. Firstly making the collective more energetically sensitive. But also making the ability to affect behavior in a positive way much more powerful. The meditation experiment in Washington was in a hot and volatile summer where the general populace was not consciously aware of it. The more mindful and actively meditative we become, the closer we come to having enough people pass the ring pass not and affecting the whole so that the collective morph to the higher vibrational energetic example. Right now the standard, in the main, is being accepted from a fear-based example. This can no longer be the case once the vibration has raised. And the tipping point of the collective has already shifted slightly from fear to love at the 2012 winter solstice.

"As the emotional climate changes on your Earth you will see many great advantages. Political systems breaking down. Old worn out ideologies crumbling and many people who are in the old consciousness destroying themselves - not able to handle the light." – The Galactic Council.

This is part of why I was urged so much to cleanse and meditate. Once the ring pass not has been passed it doesn't mean that suddenly you are walking perfection and have no problems. It just means that your filter system has been cleared sufficiently to be able to handle the intense divine and cosmic energies, without misusing the power that comes with it to satiate your base desires, ambitions and selfish agenda. You are aware of your influence on the whole and that everything is a reflection of your consciousness in a more apparent way.

"As you come to stillness, as you clear your mind, you will understand that everything is a reflection of your consciousness, of your imagination. Everything that has ever been and everything that will ever be is a reflection of your imagination, of your consciousness. All the different traditions, religious and spiritual traditions are all true, within their own paradigm of understanding. But understand that this is your imagination and your imagination is very powerful as you create this three dimensional reality. This is a holographic projection of your imagination. The holographic presentation that we have made as a collective is very real and what you create within this holographic representation once you still your mind will be up to you." – Metatron, this is the Healing Book.

All of our wonderful cultures and traditions on this planet are diverse. And the origin stories are very different in detail and characters. We have created all this and we will change it. Countries are classified by imaginary lines that have been drawn on maps. But they will only really exist while we agree to that system collectively. The more we empower ourselves into our higher creative ability, the more malleable our world becomes. We shall transcend race, religion and national identity to the greater truth of our oneness. This doesn't mean to disregard or not honor our heritage. But keeping what works and embracing our power to create a better existence. The most powerful movements that we have had from a place of identity in the past have been religious. These religions were mostly started by people who discovered their oneness and taught love and compassion. Even if they haven't been managed very well in perpetuity. The next step in our evolving society is moving away from following those who taught truth, to embodying the lesson ourselves, and using that discovered strength instead. Our power is immeasurable and when we experience this, all fear dissolves and our creativity becomes immense.

"You must concentrate on your own mastery, so that you may alleviate the suffering of the people who are panicking. The suffering of the people who are experiencing the negativity. For you, as masters, can alleviate a lot of pain and suffering. You can affect a lot of healing and make a big difference - a big impact. The true light-workers that we have mentioned - Jesus, Buddha and Krishna - have affected billions. That was only three people. You are many, and the critical mass of lightworkers that are opening up has the ability to take everybody to the next level." – Metatron, this is the Clarion Call.

I finally completed the second Galactic Council book. Just as I was finished, I went outside onto the balcony, looked into the night sky and saw four shooting stars. That was one more than I had ever seen in my entire life. It was one of the most magical moments I had ever experienced and I felt very blessed to have been able to be a part of it.

Budapest Box Begins

As was foretold, the next day we managed to secure a flat and moved into a place in Budapest we affectionately called the box. Our journey had moved on once again and our love was bringing us exactly the challenges that we needed to mould our energy into expressing our highest potential. Snowy passed away and even though we knew that it was going to happen, it was still hard. She had been with Angelina through her seminal years and was her only friend when she was being abused. In the following months we felt her with us when in meditation a lot as it sank in that she had made the transition. Some people don't understand grief for a pet and diminish the importance of it. But Snowy, even in the few months that I had known her, had touched my heart. And it felt like she had passed the baton on to me to look after her beloved Angelina.

Each different step we were making was being led by spirit. The more we let go, the deeper was the lesson of surrender. Our biggest strength was in prayer. The old adage 'The couple that prays together, stays together' was very true in our case and I realized that even though there had been times that I had prayed with other partners. It was not something that was a definite daily occurrence. I have always prayed since childhood. And it has been a comfort. But has also always focused my mind on whatever I am praying about, which resulted in a more effective outcome. It seemed that the more time we spent together, the more of an understanding of what these different disciplines and tools were for. How they worked, and how potent they could be when appreciated properly.

"It is time, your time has come. We are here to support you. In all things. We give our love to you at all times. We are multidimensional beings, here to show you your multidimensionality. We are beings connected to our source, here to show you how to connect to your source. Which is the same source. All emanate from the oneness. Recognize the power of your prayer. For when you focus on prayer (Puts hands together in prayer pose, then separates hands showing palms) What you are doing is you are taking the two halves of duality. Yin/yang, light/dark. Every duality that has come out of the oneness. And you are putting it back together with your focus (Puts hand back in prayer pose) As you focus, you create. We suggest when you pray. Once you have realized what prayer really is. That you focus on the truth of your question or intention. When you realize how powerful you really are. And you focus in prayer. There will be nothing that you cannot accomplish... NOTHING! It is time, you are ready. You are open, you are free. We are yours, in divine service. Be at peace."

The Color of Hungary

We only had a small flat in Budapest and used to give each other space in different ways. I found a great American pool hall with brand new tables and was in my element. I have always loved cue sports and started spending free time there. It was like another form of meditation and I really fell in love with the game. I had only ever played with friends before and was considered good at it. But I had not really taken it too seriously. Things were about to change. One of the owners saw me playing and asked if I would represent the club in a tournament that was coming up in a few weeks. I didn't even own a cue! So I bought one for the competition. In the majority of my past relationships, I had expressed eagerness to play but it had always been looked down upon in any serious way as a silly thing to do. I made it through the competition to play the champion of Hungary. He beat me but I could deal with that for a first competition. And I had him on the run for a lot of the match. I felt supported in my passion for the first time in my life and couldn't have been happier. It took me meeting my twin flame to realize that what my heart beats for, was the gateway to my highest potential. This isn't the only thing I love, of course, but following your highest excitement is a very important spiritual principle. And one that the Clarion Call talks about too.

"As a divine spiritual warrior of the heavenly hierarchy. You must chase whatever it is that gives you joy, that gives you bliss. Whether it be singing, dancing, acting, being a civil servant or a marine biologist. Businessman, tycoon or being in the Red Cross helping people. Everything is worthy when it is approached with passion, joy, and love, with the highest, and utmost reverence for life. This is where you may have the best life you can live"
– Metatron, this is the Clarion Call.

This was me really starting to be true to myself on a deeper level. The importance of play is not focused on enough as adults. We are children

78

of God and when life is fun and interesting, we have wide eyes and passion. We are inquisitive and enthusiastic about living life to the full. The put down "Act your age" had been thrown at me whenever I was being passionate about this kind of play before by people who saw it as a frippery. And because I do think conscientiously. It had the desired effect of putting me 'In my place'. But now that Horse had bolted and it wasn't going back in the stables.

"The highest potential of humankind can unfold most effectively with play" – The Galactic Council

I see the Merkaba and this work as a way of freeing you to be the best version of yourself. I am a free, autonomous being that has been blessed to be able to help people, through making myself as clear a channel as possible. I am not any better than anyone else. But I am just as good. I am the God force and you are too. How much we allow ourselves to access that is up to us. The Twin Flame connection helps with this because it leaves no stone unturned in our consciousness. If you are meant to be looked at as a Guru, it just means that people see you as an example of what is possible for themselves. Your true Guru is inside you. You are the Guru to yourself. It is only through trial and error with real conscious mindfulness that you will discover this. All people and things are a reflection of your consciousness and the Guru is an example of what we can all achieve. You are always Guru and Chela. Master and student. Switching roles always, and when you are ready to ascend, the reward is always greater love. The true love that transcends relationships, and is the fuel for your Merkaba. Your twin flame is one of the greatest Gurus because in the quest for them, and in the meeting of them. You are challenged to look at yourself with clear vision. If you are giving all of your power away in relationships or stealing it. The Twin Flame connection will highlight what needs to be focused on to bring you into balance. That is not always an easy path and a lot of the time you will be the Chela. If you have the humility to accept this role, you will learn quickly and ascend sooner.

Ascension - WTF is that?

What exactly is ascending? With all of the different people and groups promoting Ascension. There are many takes on what that means. It can be confusing as to what is really going on. Especially when first starting out on this journey. There are so many different opinions. And because of the passion that people embody when they first awaken. It can seem like it reinforces the effects of the ego instead of diminishing it. That passion is great but the most powerful thing is always working on yourself instead of just trying to change the world. The world changes more rapidly when we work on our own consciousness than anything else. Our peace and the love that we emanate multiplies the energy which empowers people, unlike proselytizing. When the energy is pure, people are inspired and led to follow the feeling and teaching instead of just the teacher. That is where the real magic lies.

Spiritual ascension is the recognition, awareness, and ability to practically apply the blessings that come with understanding, and ultimately experiencing that we are all one energy system. When this is experienced, inner and outer peace follow as a result. This has been happening to individuals for thousands of years. Ascension for mankind is the reaching of a critical mass of people who have had this experience. The knock on effect of this is world peace, complete global enlightenment and a society that reflects that state of being.

Ascension is on many levels. Our **Technological Ascension** is in full swing and the world is rapidly changing in this way. Moore's law stated that technology would double every eighteen months to two years. This is not really a law, but more of a prediction by Gordon Moore, the guy that started Intel. Stating that the number of transistors that can fit on a microchip would double every two years or so. It has become a belief about all advancements in technology. It was only a prediction for a ten year period in 1965 and yet it has held pretty accurately for over 50 years now and shows no signs of stopping. What this means is that we are getting pretty advanced by our recent standards. And science fiction is increasingly becoming science fact. If we can go from Horse and cart to space flight in less than a hundred years. Just imagine what we can do if technology keeps doubling at this rate.

Our **Societal Ascension** is also in full swing and rapidly accelerating. It has moved forward in leaps and bounds in the last 50 years also with the conscious awareness of human rights, women's rights and the civil rights movement being an essential part of the zeitgeist. The more aware we are of what is actually going on in different parts of the world. The easier it will be for us as a collective to discern the best path forward. The 1% vs 99% understanding, occupy movement and truth revealers or "Whistleblowers" that have emerged are all raising awareness of what is actually going on and who is and isn't benefitting. People are growing in dissatisfaction with the status quo and the more the truth is brought into view, the more we are inspired and motivated to make changes.

"The organizational structures that have kept you in ignorance have relied greatly on that ignorance. It has been their main strength. For when any group of people needs to keep secrets and tell you it is to protect you, it is really to protect themselves from their schemes and plans. And from the hierarchy and the families of the hierarchies that are in place on your Earth plane from being prosecuted. Those who believe that they are above the law shall be subject to their own karma. The more you move forward towards a transparent society, the fairer your society will become and the reasons for these secrets being kept will not be there anymore. For when a system is open to proper scrutiny from the whole, it comes into alignment with divine justice and your own innate sense of fairness. It is always the minority amongst you that wishes to control the majority and wishes to not be held accountable for their actions. All will be held accountable for their actions. For all is coming into the light dear ones." – The Galactic Council.

The Galactic Council puts it that we are graduating. That the graduation classes are over the next fifty years.

"You shall know the truth, and the truth shall set you free." - John 8:32

We are becoming more and more consciously aware that we are programmable. **Mental Ascension** is de-programming ourselves from old, disempowering, controlling structures of thought and discovering our true potential. Our abilities are immense but our collective beliefs are many times limiting and obstructing our happiness and peace.

"Recognize the power of your words. The power of your programming. For this is what words do, they program you. And recognizing that you have autonomy over which words you assimilate within your being will free you to create the life that you wish to have, instead of settling for the life that others have used words to create within you. The more wisely you choose your reading materials, the faster your transformation. Also in choosing how you express yourself wisely. This is a very powerful key to your transformation. You have the power to affect many others with your words, every individual that you come into contact with when you are being mindful of your speech and discerning in the assimilation of the words you hear. Recognize the patterns of the words you hear from others. Whether they are on a loop of hypnosis from others or whether they are deliberately projecting their words to you or to others. Avoid the beings who are deliberately projecting negative, vitriol, gossip, hatred etc. Actively seek the company of those who use their words wisely in love, in empowerment, and in peace. And deliberately project upon those caught in cycles of hypnosis and conditioning, positive messages, positive transformational words. The word is the key to your transformation in its current state. As you transcend the

different levels of consciousness and ascend much higher in your evolution. Words will be of no importance. As you will communicate on much deeper levels. However, at this stage of your development. Recognize, appreciate and utilize your words as effectively and succinctly as you possibly can." - The Galactic Council.

We were moving through the different levels of de-programming together and many cycles were still in play. I had come to my experience of oneness many years ago and yet could still feel my Fathers energy through some of my expression. This was fine in the good ways that he had programmed me. But a lot of it was lower energy. His rage, most probably a programmed reality from his own upbringing, could still be detected by me. I didn't let it manifest in the physical but could feel it rising at times. Anger is so destructive. And part of what I believe gave him so many heart attacks. He had his first one at age 40. The year that I was born. He had six altogether, not counting the ones he had as he passed away. The biggest problem in my opinion with regards to this was his feelings of righteousness about this aspect of his personality. He was 'Godly' in this expression, in his opinion.

"The wrath of God comes upon the sons of disobedience." - Ephesians 5:6

The red mist was something that I had become, as much as possible, adept at avoiding in him when I was a child. He genuinely tried to do the right thing mostly but "children were to be seen and not heard" was a belief that he had, and "You do as I say, not as I do" was a favorite saying of his also, and his word was law.

In the last year of his life. When Mum was going through her Chemo. While I was being tested to the limit to try and keep peace and calm in the house. We had an incident. His stress was at a max and I could feel the anger rising in him. I could feel the volatility of all the pressure rising within me too. Mum was such a sensitive soul that she could feel, well in advance, any altercations arising. I didn't always understand what was happening in my childhood in the way that she acted. It was such a deep sensitivity that I have only now, in meeting Angelina, been graced with the same deeply sensitive, feminine, empathic force. This was showing me parallels now that I felt were important to pay heed to. My dad lost his temper at some flippant comment I made and instantly started punching me in the chest and stomach over and over. Even though he was older, he was still as strong as an ox with his anger. As well as the rage, there was so much fear, emotional pain, and anguish because of my Mums illness. In feeling this deeper energy, I somehow managed to stand and take it without stopping him, only guarding my face. I just absorbed his punches and emotional rage and didn't make a sound. I took my part of responsibility in the event because I realized that it was just an outlet for frustration. This was very confusing to him and he just stopped, spent and empty of rage. I believe that I was empowered, once again, by Archangel Michael at that moment. It was the last time that he ever hit me and a calm came over the house afterward that I had never experienced before. I never saw him angry again after that day.

I remembered this as the anger came up to be cleared within me. As twin flames proceed on their path together, what surfaces is sometimes what you think is fully dealt with. The speck of dirt on a 20w light-bulb cannot be seen as well as on a 60w. The more light you hold, the greater the intensity of sensitivity. And what needs to be dealt with becomes clearer. It was a very potent moment in my journey. The recognition of our cellular memory and the ability to clear it is a very powerful tool for transformation in our awakening.

My dad's programming was very deeply ingrained. And because of this, his triggers to violence as a solution were touch sensitive. This is an important point with regards to our **Societal Ascension**. Because those who would oppress us cannot do so without our collective agreement in the system. Our individual triggers, if we are present enough to face them. Are an important key to global transformation. If we don't participate in a paradigm, we don't actively perpetuate it. Leaving us free to create other, better systems.

"You are being provoked; you are being provoked towards violence. And in this state it is very easy for those who would oppress you, to dominate you. It is

important to recognize this provocation for what it is. For civil war is still war and while you engage in it. While you do the bidding of those who are manipulating you. Whether that is serving to further the cause of financial elites or rising up in violence against them with a uniform or without a uniform is still engaging, indulging and participating in a paradigm that is ready to change.

Although there has been much great service by those who wear a uniform. Believing that they are defending something. This paradigm is no longer the case. Your merkabas are much greater weapons than what is put in your hands in order to kill others. Your merkabas will switch you into the frequency where you do not need to indulge in these things, where you do not need to participate in this paradigm. It will help you change the paradigm so that your Fathers, Sons, Brothers, Daughters, Sisters, and Mothers do not have to go to war with a uniform or without a uniform. War will be obsolete in your physical existence. Do not allow yourself to be provoked. Change your frequency, change your vibration and create the world without violence in any of its forms.

You are powerful enough to do this already with a simple change of your mindset. But when you open your merkaba, you will help to bring this change upon the Earth plane. And help to influence the whole world. Nobody has to die in this way anymore. Nobody wants to die in this way anymore. This is not a situation that has to continue. Come into alignment with your divine being and teach your Children valuable lessons that will not include violence of any kind." - The Galactic Council.

I was feeling the initial lessons of my childhood coming up strongly and trying to take a step back and look at things objectively. Seeing the motivation behind my parents and those who I had around me at that time. Scrutinizing my own actions and belief systems that were a result of this programming and what I was deliberately acting upon of my own volition. We were increasingly discussing the possibility of having our own children. I had already had a hand in raising a few kids and was reviewing how much of that parenting was influenced by the tone and beliefs of my parents.

"The children of your Earth must become your greatest priority. For all your actions are teaching your children. You must scrutinize your actions and your belief systems in order to realize what it is that you are teaching your children. For you are always teaching your children, no matter whose progeny they are. You are shaping the World by every decision that you make and every decision you make is teaching your children." The Galactic Council.

Your inner child is just as important as the children growing now. All the unresolved issues that you have from your childhood need your love and attention. But you also need to nurture the child that is still there. The silenced boy or girl that wants to play, that wants to make friends. That wants your love. Releasing your ego and allowing yourself to have fun sends out a homing signal. A beacon to your playmate. Your Twin Flame. It signals the return to innocence and empowerment that only kids can give you. No kid is born hating or judging. But because their vulnerability has been prayed upon in many different ways, it has closed down the fun and silenced the voice. In being brave enough to be silly, we open that voice back up. And the inherent fairness and joy of childhood returns once again. As an adult child, you are more empowered and less susceptible to abuse. You are a warrior child now. Standing in your innocent power and aware that all abuse is, in some ways, a cry for more love and nurturing.

Twin flame crucible

Each time we surrendered to the divine path and experienced an ego death, the testing was more pronounced. Our small flat in Budapest became the coziest, comfy and intimate space. We were full of tantric delight with a passion beyond imagining. Lost in each other's essence and flesh for days on end. But also, as this depth intensified, so did the moments of insecurity and the runner dynamic trying to rip us apart. Unconsciously but then obviously searching and sifting through each part of our lives. Exploring the motives that were left behind by different characters in our individual stories that had left a negative impression. Our egos were dining on the scraps. The remnants of our other, less divinely focused relationships.

People who have come through difficult abuse can be hyper-aware of the dual nature of people. How someone can be very plausible, personable and feel safe one moment. And then be sneaky and destructive the next. This obvious abuse, and the contemplation of it, when on the conscious spiritual path, gets flipped back into self-reflection. And, when completely transparent and intent on spiritual advancement, a very powerful tool for transformation. We are all susceptible to this abusive duality when we are not operating from our source, no matter how subtly it manifests within us. The degree we allow this dual part of our personality to be scrutinized depends on our brutal honesty and degree of humility.

We were going through periods of total oneness one moment to being in deep duality and dysfunction the next. The intensity of our play expanded and with the bliss of an ever-expanding heart came deep vulnerability. When stuck in this illusion, the experience was like a lucid nightmare. Each different point of breaking down our ego was like poking a raw nerve on a rotten tooth with a pin. Each time an ego death happened, the never-ending templates of potential increased. The intensity of the bond is so powerful that it breaks down all imperfections that obstruct you from your god-self. And when in our Tantric embrace, our God-self was all there was, pure transcendent bliss. The negativity is perfectly designed to highlight what needs to be changed within the subtle templates of your transformation. Each time we let go to the light in prayer and acceptance of the fallibility of the flesh with Ho'oponopono, we were brought back into balance. The intensity of this was so potent that it resulted in great clarity.

Amrita Awareness Drive

The Galactic Council books were talking about the next stage of our evolution. That we are capable of accessing a substance they refer to as divine nectar. That our physical essence is changing and something cosmic is happening to our bodies. That this isn't just an attitudinal, emotional and spiritual shift. But that we are in the middle of a physical evolutionary leap also. It's easy to imagine what could happen in thousands of years when we think about how species evolve incrementally through natural selection. Each different development fulfilling a necessary purpose brought about by a need to adapt to the changing environment.

"Crises are the energetic catalysts of evolution" – The Galactic Council

In a global time for our species of mass starvation, ecological suicide in an ecosystem ill-equipped for abuse on such a massive scale. And a death machine consisting of our own self-destruction through war, chemicals and the almighty god of money. The stress of such an environment and our awareness of it is speeding up our evolutionary adaptational necessity. Twenty thousand children dying of starvation daily in a world with plenty of food is a hard statistic to know about without feeling stressed. And nature is making us adapt for the continuance of the species. Instead of us developing abilities to help with fight or flight. We are being made aware of the cumulative effects of our physical evolution in our hidden ability to feed ourselves straight from the source.

"These books are about the most advanced point of mastery you can achieve within a Human vessel in this

lifetime." The Galactic Council.

I was a little incredulous and overwhelmed after channeling these books and started researching the different concepts. I came across a documentary about Breatharianism, Sungazing and Cosmic feeding around the world. In this documentary was a chap called Prahlad Jani. A Holy man from India who claimed to have not eaten or drunk anything for decades after a process was activated within him that fed him directly from the source. This seemed to confirm what the books were talking about. They tested this chap for ten days under medical and video supervision. He didn't eat, drink, urinate or defecate for a ten-day period. Scans revealed that a liquid substance appeared in his stomach that was reabsorbed into his body. His brain scans showed the brain of a twenty-five-year-old, even though this guy is in his seventies. He spends most of his time doing yoga and depends on no-one. The doctors said that if he was found to be a fraud that they would reveal it to the world. But after the study was complete, they were left scratching their heads.

In Paramahansa Yogananda's book 'Autobiography of a Yogi' a similar story was relayed about a yogi called Giri Bala who asked the divine to take away her greed. She spent a similar lifetime without food, according to the book.

The longest that I had fasted was 79 days when I did the Clarion Call. But I had never envisioned it being a permanent thing before. Having always thought about it in terms of clearing and cleansing. Increasingly I felt more and more comfortable when there was nothing in my stomach. I always had support though. It was always some type of juice fast. This was not really a fast at all that they were describing. It is a secretion of the pineal gland that contains all that we need to not only survive but thrive.

This concept was hard to swallow at first for me, pardon the pun. From our finite physical perspective. But then I started thinking about where anything comes from and how little we know about it. The big bang is a scientific theory we understand from the laws of physics, reversing the expansion we see in the universe to a single point. But when you think about the concept, it actually sounds more spiritual and supernatural than scientific. A big bang exploded into matter and everything that we can observably measure in the almost 14 billion years of expansion since then, came from this explosion - that was smaller than the size of a pinhead! Just this theory in itself makes the concept of divine nectar sound very possible. Where would it come from? Well, where did anything come from? The truth is that the greatest scientific minds of our species so far cannot definitively answer that question yet. I love this because it brings wonder and excitement back into the equation.

"Your incredulity at all these concepts will fade when you test these theories out. We do not ask for blind faith. We do not tell you what to believe. We merely present the truth to you and we challenge you to discover these things for yourself. If you keep an open mind and you allow yourself to challenge what you have been told to believe in. If you have the courage to break the chains of perceived wisdom, you will rapidly move forward. And if you put these things into practice, you will truly have the life of your dreams, and you will be called a master." - The Galactic Council.

What's the point?

The greatest importance of all of these teachings to me was the way they made me feel. Did it matter if I was going to board a flying saucer, set off for the stars and be living from divine nectar? What really mattered was the positive change they made to my every-day life and relationships. How every day I am told that these books have changed peoples lives for the better. The disciplines that I've been led to over the years have made me a fitter, healthier and more balanced individual. My path has led me to the most beautiful girl in the world, that genuinely loves me for who I am. She looks at me like I am a magical being. And I really do believe she is magical too.

These philosophies have brought me a sense of wonder and the manifestation of many divine friendships. Adventures to realms that I didn't even know existed. And to countries, I never thought I would visit. The practical application of meditation, prayer, yoga and conscious fuelling, has completely transformed my life. Healed me and given me a sense of confidence I never previously had. And if I can do it, anybody can. I think that is the reason I was chosen for this work. Because I am an average guy. The center on the spectrum of humanities abilities. But even as an average Joe. I still feel ahead of my game when I am applying these philosophies and disciplines faithfully. And this is all a game. The great game of life and how you play it is up to you. If you choose to love and to aim higher, the world is your oyster.

"Each different being on your Earth is capable of rapid expansion in every different way." – The Galactic Council.

I started to get excited about the idea of really traveling in a spaceship. Part of me was still dismissing this as a reality, even after having the experience of channeling the books and bi-locating to Orion. My human, 'rational' self, was still thinking that maybe I was just a little bit eccentric, creative and fanciful. What evidence was there of crafts anyway. I remembered a part in the first Galactic Council book.

"The lights over Phoenix and many mass sightings that have happened lately will be happening more frequently and are serving to bring you into your realization of the truth of extra terrestrial life forms. We are making it increasingly obvious." – The Galactic Council.

I found a documentary about it with many eyewitnesses and footage of what they were talking about. On the night of March 13th, 1997 a V-shaped collection of lights were seen over Phoenix, Arizona that defied any rational explanation that was given by 'official' sources. The Arizona Governor at the time held a press conference because it had been reported by thousands of people. And he claimed that he knew who was responsible. He had a man dressed in an alien suit come out to ridicule and make light of the whole thing. Years later he admitted to having seen it himself. There was an investigation launched and over 700 witnesses were interviewed.

"All great truths go through three stages. First they are ridiculed, then they are opposed and finally they are accepted as self evident." - Anon

Kurt Russell, the famous actor, was one of the witnesses. But only remembered the event years later. Relaying the story on the Graham Norton show on the BBC in the UK in April 2017. He said he was flying a friend to Phoenix in his private plane when they both saw the lights and couldn't explain what they were. He called it in and once he landed, recorded it in his flight logbook.

"We are being very sensitive to your people. We are being very sensitive to the whole of humanity for we do not wish to spread any fear. We do not wish to cause any anxiety. There is enough anxiety and fear on your Earth plane already without us adding to it. We are here to lift you up; we are here to expand your awareness so that you might seek contact more and more." – The Galactic Council.

HeartGasms

The deeper we went in Tantric connection and meditation, the more profound the feeling when we were together. And it seemed like we were together, even when we were apart. It was surreal in the way that the sensual physical experience was becoming more meditative in the way the energy rose, resulting in full body tantric pulsing orgasms from the heart. But exploding out in all directions. Our third eyes in synch with visions we experienced while in an embrace and in the astral lucid dream state coinciding at times perfectly. We were a double ourorobus, complete and at peace. Infinity manifesting in the physical experience.

These heartgasms were a pulsing fuel for our merkabas. This is the biggest realization concerning Spiritual Ascension. Once enough people have a real understanding of what the Merkaba is, how to use it, and that it is not just an abstract woo-woo nonsense. The world will rapidly advance. Love has been seen as weakness, a vulnerability. But in its purest sense, when utilized properly, is the most empowering, powerful and transformational thing there is. When your Merkaba is being fuelled purely and exercised regularly with discipline and commitment, reality becomes pliable. And the interval between thought and manifestation becomes less. This is why the ring pass not is so important. The focus being on impeccability and service means that once you are able to harness the power and consciously materialize with it, you are aware of the responsibility that this tool comes with.

"Once you truly pass the Ring Pass Not, you will not abuse this tool. You will have no wish to abuse this tool. But in understanding that <u>you are</u> the riches of the universe, you will not crave the same things that you crave when you are gripped by the lower chakras. For you will understand that you are supported by all, and you can create all. And manifest whatever you desire and be at one with your consciousness.

Thanks have to always be given. In other words, you have to be in a frame of mind of gratitude that there is a continuum of wonderful abundance, and your Merkaba will manifest all that you desire and all that you wish to help others.

This is a powerful tool, the most powerful tool that you can ever have. Respect this understanding, and you will be taken to higher heights." - Metatron, this is the Clarion Call.

This existence is a template we have agreed to collectively and set in motion individually in order to experience subjective expansion. According to my guides, you have agreed to your physical body and the family you have been incarnated with. Certain parameters that have been cultivated through circumstance within this incarnation are also important for what you are to address or help with your Twin Flame and their mission. What you do within these parameters becomes less restricted the more you expand the awareness of your higher self with your Merkaba.

As you connect with your Twin Flame. All of your bad habits, negative traits, and cycles of unhelpful behavior come into the spotlight over and over. These things will keep repeating in a loop and your twin flame will have the perfect response to show your rational self the mirror you need to make changes. If you have no intention of making a change or addressing problems, it will become untenable. It will be a nightmare and your vibrations will clash in such a way as to make it obvious that you have the ability to change the situation. This is your opportunity to defeat your ego. If your ego holds firm and you do not surrender to your higher self, you will not be able to remain together. Your greatest potential can be reached in each other's aura. The pure guidance of the twin flame is benevolent and sees beyond the illusion.

"You have nothing to fear apart from old habits of self-destruction. Of allowing others to manipulate your energy and lead you down paths of destruction, Hold firm to the love inside, for you are the God force." – The Galactic Council.

In your twin flames aura, if you are being humble in your approach, you will quickly see beneficial results. And the shift in frequency will highlight the patterns of behavior that are defeating you. I was completely lifted from my environment in Scotland. The prophecy had been eagerly awaited and when the time came I jumped in with both feet. The results from this were swift and my body and attitude changed almost overnight. I can see why this happened to me so dramatically as the systems of comfort, support and old patterning were, a lot of the time, just laziness and lack of dynamism on my own part. When I was taken completely out of my comfort zone and challenged to create new, more intensely committed realities. My potential became much more obvious to me and I could see very clearly the systems of energy that had been holding me back.

Return of the Djedi

The stories from the Star Wars films, according to the Clarion Call, were channeled. The recognition of our humanity and capacity for great good or evil being played out. Our 'Fall' from grace and enduring our own karma are ancient concepts packaged in a fun way. There were supposedly ancient Egyptian warriors called the Djedi that guarded the Pharaoh. Imbued with ancient knowledge of alchemy and 'The force'. These ancient teachings were of the column of light and the kundalini. How to raise the energies and what to do with the subsequent abilities that arose with the flow being fully grounded. The teachings were buried and deliberately quashed to be rediscovered and resurrected later by the Templar Knights. The deep truth and purity of the knights was very important because of the power that came with these teachings. This became what was taught in mystery schools and that esoteric knowledge is now becoming exoteric in it's wider presentation. These films are a way of us seeing the power within ourselves and how we can harness it. There are many ascension films and each time we resonate with a concept, we are being awoken to the deeper truth of ourselves.

The Father issue within the story is a powerful illustration of our patterning and ability to overcome what we have become or are being manipulated to become. The patriarchy and heavy abuse of masculine power are highlighted strongly within these stories. The task is of us coming into balance in the force of masculine and feminine within us. The Twin Flame dynamic cannot coexist without both parties fully stepping into their divine roles. Each different coupling will have their own specific power dynamic that they have to address. But the power is in surrender and intuition. Being humble enough to let the stronger intuition lead. And recognizing that the power lies in what is right rather than who is right. Masculine and Feminine in this regard are not gender specific within the deeper energy of the Twin Flame alchemy. However the patterns and assigned roles play a big part in understanding what needs addressed within.

The masculine abuse of power is heavily entrenched in religious dialogue and this programming has been happening for millennia in our own society.

"Simon Peter said to them: "Let Mary go out from our midst, for Women are not worthy of life!" Jesus says: "See, I will draw her so as to make her male so that she also may become a living spirit like you males. For every woman who has become male will enter the kingdom of heaven." - Gospel of Thomas V I I4

Societal Ascension is addressing this at a growing rate and the courage to face the structure and attitudes of our world is beginning to take shape. The divine masculine is being called upon within the ascension process to address himself with more scrutiny. It's easy to be in the place of power privilege and assert that there is no problem. To be in that place and act from your divine core in complete integrity to affect change, is the challenge of the divine masculine now.

Shiva & Shakti up a tree k.i.s.s.i.n.g

Shiva and Shakti is the divine dance of masculine and feminine within the Universe. When in a divine relationship, the Shakti is the feminine emotional chaos that can only be brought into balance by the masculine Shiva certainty of solid unconditional love. This energy, when manifest within the Twin Flame relationship, is the most optimizing of forces. It can only be fully honored in humility and selfless surrender to the divine within. Shakti will test Shiva to the deepest limits of his sincerity, loyalty and the consistency of his abilities and convictions. Shiva and Shakti are inherent within each individual. And the extent of the need to balance these within us will manifest according to the particular traits of each person. Shiva is pure consciousness and needs Shakti energy to make creation. Shakti is pure energy and needs Shiva to make optimum use of it. Only with the union of the two in balance can your potential be fulfilled.

I was being urged to be in my divine masculine power more and more as issues came up to be cleared. The chaotic Shakti manifesting within Angelina in every different way to trigger me was a testing force that I didn't realize could be so challenging. Our personal trigger points were being pushed to the limit, the more we moved into our mastery. The more focused the intensity, the more the subtleties of being out of alignment were highlighted. Holding myself in the deepest mastery, at this level, seemed much easier when I was fasting. During these times the awareness of my personal Shiva energy came through me and I felt the rising levels of mastery bringing me into an ascending state of divine oneness and healing. My service was much more effective and everything became easier to manifest. Ego and oneness were side by side jockeying for position within me as each time I cleansed I could see more clearly what needed to be worked upon to help with the divine path we were both on together.

I was told that in this detachment and accepting my role as divine masculine within the situation, that my fullest and purest potential could be reached. This vision was still sinking in of all my wildest dreams becoming a reality when our situation changed once again.

Magnificent Malta Magic

Our contract was up on the flat in Budapest and the next step of our journey was undecided. We felt America calling but were not sure how this was going to happen. The Galactic Council had mentioned a few different places as being important to concentrate on. The closest of these was the island of Malta.

"Malta – Is a place of great divine transformation. It is a central point for much of what is happening in this half of the globe. There is an inter-dimensional portal here that can access every different part of your Earth."** – The Galactic Council.

As well as being relevant for ascension, it was also the childhood place Angelina resonated with the most. This was before her abuse and was only a few hours plane trip, so we packed up and headed off.

The silent lightning in Malta is one of the most amazing things I have ever experienced. The sky dancing for hours, but not a whisper of thunder. It was like God playing us our own amazing movie and the channeling of divine experiences became even more intense. As I sat in meditation during the silent, heavenly, light displays. I was shown the pregnancy of the Earth. The cosmic eggs ready to hatch of the awakening beings, opening to their most empowered reality. The intensity of the sky and the way the telepathic waves were behaving was transcendent and grounding at the same time. I was shown how the political uncertainty of the future global stage was being used as a catalyst for awakening. The polarity of our consciousness deepening in darkness, just before the dawn. And the light of illumination finally showing us all the truth.

We were facing the direction of Palestine from our flat. And the lightning, illuminating the sky, was opening my consciousness more and more. What was the significance of this place? We were over twelve hundred miles away from the Palestinian coast. But there was only sea separating us.

Years ago, a few months before I fully opened my Merkaba for the first time. I had a brief experience of what felt like plugging into the Earth. I had drawn the scene at the time and written what had happened at the side of the drawing.

"As I lifted my arms, it came through me and dispersed all over the World. Lighting up what looked like chicken wire in different layers, and different colors. The shapes becoming smaller and smaller all over the globe in a big network of tiny capillaries. I felt like I had just plugged into the planet. Feeling joy and voices of everyone and everything, and a sense of having arrived. Like I was ready for something, but I didn't know what."

I was feeling the same thing now and with every flash of lightning, it was dispersing power and connection to each different place on the globe. The point of the Dome of the Rock in Jerusalem was being highlighted in my mind as a place of important focus for humanity. Why did this place keep coming up? Why was it so important, and why now?

"The Dome of the Rock in Jerusalem –

This is a point of much conflict over the centuries, much claiming and reclaiming. It will be used in political maneuvering to enflame and try to escalate a war on your Earth plane. It is the most religiously sensitive place on your Earth plane. And although it is volatile and has been volatile, this is nothing for you to fear. This is another important place for you to visit in your merkabas, to help bring peace to the area. This is a place of great inspiration and there are many different species that are helping awaken mankind through this sensitive spot. It is a place of great epiphany, not just in travelling there physically, but also in opening up your consciousness and relating to the conflict that has happened around this area." - The Galactic Council.

As I connected to this beautiful place of inspiration. And the flashes of lightning continued in front of me. Great flashes of epiphany struck me also. This conflict wasn't just about religion, politics, money, oil, control and power. This was about the balance of masculine and feminine on the planet. The centuries of imbalance and misuse of masculine power in violence, dominance, and manipulating the trigger points of personal identification.

The significance of this place is because it is the focus of mental identification with billions of people who happen to be born as Christians, Muslims, and Jews. That is over half of the people on Earth! And it is only in connecting with the same spirit that is within all of these people, that peace will be reached.

As lightworkers, one of the fundamental understandings is that the labels given at birth are only temporary ones. To be worked through and transcended. The significance of this area being a point of transformation through the ring-pass-not on a global scale is to do with prophecy. Because we create our own reality, and until we become conscious of this fact, our reality is influenced by the beliefs, traditions and prophesies of our forefathers. Only when we transcend that programmed identification and trigger point to reaction, can we move through the conditioning and start to create fully from choice. Until then we will be actively, consciously or not, trying to fulfill the prophecy laid down before us.

"Each part of your journey is mathematically precise. But every single move is not predetermined. Every single move is determined upon the level of vibration that you are emitting. You have great creative control over your experience." – The Galactic Council.

As we face the imbalances given to us by our familial, religious and societal conditioning. We come into the balance of our Merkaba. This is when it can open fully, we pass the ring-pass-not and our power to create expands. Many of these beautiful cosmic eggs of consciousness that I was seeing, were ready to hatch. And many more were being incubated to hatch at a later date.

These eggs are within all people at different stages. Many people who are stuck in deep hatred and conditioned hypnosis are ready to hatch. This is why it is important to not judge anyone. Because this wonderful game does not make it obvious who is ready to wake up.

The flat we rented was in St Pauls Bay. Named after the apostle Paul from the Bible, who was shipwrecked on the island while on his way to be tried for political rebellion. Paul was a cosmic egg who's time had come. Before he was an apostle, and long before he was on Malta. He was on the road to Damascus, on his way to persecute Christians, when he had an awakening experience. Suddenly filled with divine fire, he became a holy force of healing and love.

Malta was one of the first places in the Roman Kingdom to convert to

Christianity. The story goes that Paul was bitten by a poisonous snake there, but suffered no illness. This was taken as a sign by the islanders that he was special. And later, he healed the Father of Publius, the top Roman on the island. Publius converted to Christianity and became the first Bishop in the country. This decorative symbolism in Malta was very evident.

The snake symbolism was pertinent as we had raised our kundalini and were continuing to expand it together. Manifestation was becoming more powerful, and as we surrendered to God in tantric bliss, mystical things were happening again. I was playing pool one evening when a millionaire businessman from the Netherlands asked about the Hebrew tattoos on my arm. The symbols are very powerful and precious to me. They are three of the seventy-two names of God in the Kabbalah and mean 'Absolute certainty in the power of God', 'Healing' and 'Miracles'. After finding this out, he started talking about how he had trained in meditation and been on long fasting retreats that brought him into great manifestation consciousness. A collector of rare spiritual and religious artifacts, he makes a fortune in various businesses. And always gives away half of the money he makes as a way of repaying the divine for the blessings he has received.

He recounted a story, with great gravitas, of a powerful stone he acquired from a mysterious sage. This wise old man told him to pass it on, when the time was right, to a chosen one he would synchronistically meet. To get the stone, they had to travel into the Hoia-Baciu forest in Transylvania, on a full moon, at midnight. It was buried in a hidden cave, deep in the forest. He said it was the most frightening experience he'd ever had. As they approached the cave, the hairs went up all over his body with what seemed like supernatural electricity. The old man said that the stone had been delivered some decades before, from another world. And he had been entrusted with it. As they took the stone from a glowing, futuristic looking box. He saw a green pulse of energy escaping. The old man turned to him, put the stone into his hand, and shouted "RUN!". They both ran as fast as they could, out of the forest. He felt like they were being chased all the way. And as they managed to get into the clearing, with the lights of the waiting car and the Moon, a blood curdling wail was heard echoing into the night. And the old man disappeared, never to be seen again.

This was all very dramatic and he was definitely a charismatic storyteller. He said I was to have it and asked his wife to fetch the stone from their hotel room. Handing me the stone, he suggested I cut it into pieces. As I held it, I felt a very strong vibration. Like the moldavite effect, but more powerful. It felt like it was talking to me. Another form of tektite, but much bigger than any tektite I'd ever had before. I said I liked the feeling of it in one piece. He replied that the old man told him that when it was split in three, that the fullest functions of it would be activated. And it would have found it's place and purpose. He left with his family and for the rest of the night, I held the stone, feeling a beautiful energy flow.

For the next week or so, I had the stone with me constantly and was really enjoying the powerful vibe I got with it. As with the pieces of Moldavite I've had over the years. This stone seemed very transformational. I kept thinking about cutting it up and what the old man had said. What if it was not meant for me? What if I was meant to pass it to someone else? I didn't want to do anything to it just in case. I wanted to honor the stone as it felt very special. Just as I was thinking this, I accidentally dropped it on the floor and it split into three pieces.

The next day we discovered that the family carer for Angelinas Mama had put her in an old folks home in Hungary and left the country with the pets unattended. We packed up and left Malta on a pet rescue mission. Happily, Mama was being very well cared for and much happier and better off where she was. But the pets had been left in a terrible state. We had them transported back to Spain and jumped on a plane.

On the first of the first 2017, we moved into flat 5D on the 5th floor of a beach front apartment in Estepona, Spain. We were living in 5D at last. This was only a few weeks after I had the mystical stone in my hand. Things have always tended to move quickly when I get that transformative feeling. Since meeting Angelina, it has accelerated and each time it happens, we quickly find ourselves in a different location, with a different set of challenges and energies. With so much talk of what it means to be living in 5D. I had a constant reminder now to try to expand my awareness and mastery each time I saw my door number.

I was being shown more about prophecy and how timelines are set in motion. That we were living in a time of a prophecy of Christ consciousness being fulfilled. And that this was an inevitable thing on the road of spiritual consciousness. Each species that evolve to this point, experiences breaking out of the cosmic egg. And each different heart that opens to unconditional love, accelerates the Golden age being manifested. A new symbolism was brought into my readings with my work at this time, of the Dandelion. This is about deliberate creation and being clear from the controlling mental influence of others. This is a symbol of the toroidal field at it's most powerful, and a very important understanding.

Toroidal Field Theory

Within the individualized information system that you are, you have your own toroidal field. This is what is seen clairvoyantly as your Aura. It is the flow of all of the information of your existence and how it is organized within your experience. It moves around and through your four-body system. Everyone has this flow. Without it, you cannot exist. When you activate your Merkaba consciously, you expand your ability to access the information within your field with more clarity. This comes with a feeling of expansion and greater awareness. You also tap into the whole energy system of the flower of life. This means that the information flow expands and you have more access to the greater toroidal field of infinite awareness - what some call the Akashic records. This doesn't always happen all at once. But as you clear the blocks in your chakras and raise your kundalini, the flow becomes more apparent. The clearer you become, the more access you have to this information. And the more spiritual power you have access to consciously. The Merkaba is the way you open up to your toroidal field. All spiritual traditions that have unconditional love as a central tenet help you open up the access to your toroidal field. The more freedom you have to create within any ideology, the closer it is to the truth of explaining existence. And the more it will benefit you on your path of **spiritual ascension.**

"Whenever you are being told not to look at other belief systems, to only believe what you are being told, you are not being respected and your inner light is not being allowed to shine. The validity of any teaching is in what it creates and how much it frees you to be the better version of you. Anything that encourages you to be subservient to the will of that which you are being told exists without being allowed to research it is merely a system of control." – The Galactic Council.

The experience of coming into the zero point empowers you to recognize that there will always be a point of control. It either comes from outside of us in the form of ideology, rules and belief systems from others that we subscribe to or allow. Or it comes from within in the form of enlightenment, self-realization, and mastery. Our experience is a pathway of growth and each different experience we have is always perfect to facilitate our deepest awakening. Every complex system of spiritual truth contains red herrings to deter those unready or insincere. The onus is on us to sharpen our senses to what the divine is showing us from moment to moment so that we start to use our divine control point to create.

"Your creative potential is unlimited and as you open up your synapses through connection to your higher source, to the Christ grid. You utilize the full range of your capabilities. Moving from fear to love changes all things. And in this next stage of your understanding you will take your own breath away in the realization of your own magnificence." - The Galactic Council.

Each pair of Twin Flames will have their perfect antagonism as well as perfect complimentary aspects for growth. Angelinas O.C.D meant that I had to become more sensitive to the impact order has on surroundings and mental peace. O.C.D affects 2% of the population. That is over 14 million people. Leonardo DiCaprio and Charlize Theron both suffer from this anxiety and lead very successful lives. The repetitive nature of it, when consciously used to best advantage, brings you into a very focused place if you are able to stay mindful as a partner. I was learning deeper consideration and patience.

The divine masculine is being called upon to support the rise of the divine feminine. To facilitate the empowerment of the oppressed and bring humanity into balance in a divine way at last. The oppression of the feminine within men as well as all women in general within society is being addressed. This is one of the biggest reasons for Twin Flames being brought together at this time. Because the imbalance has been so severe and competitive that men have been drilled, shamed and brainwashed into closing their hearts. The abuse of the masculine energy has impacted men severely. Their bravery in war is now being called upon for ascension.

De Oppresso Liber – From being oppressed to being free.

And the battle plan is a jihad of internal transformation, as well as standing in power to not accept or participate with, in any way, the misogynistic narrative from other men. And having the strength of character and love for their fellow man to not dominatingly ridicule their awakening. The holy war is upon us and the enemy is our own ego and legacy from the past. The divine feminine has always been called to love and nurture others and is also being called to service. To hold space for the divine masculine to open his heart to love completely. Women have been systematically vilified by church and state for centuries in obvious and subtle ways and this is now being faced and healed. In being sensitive, patient and kind with each other, we will lay the foundation for the biggest transformation mankind has ever seen.

"This is the seventh time we have participated in the transformation of consciousness of a species on the Earth. You have been by far the most entertaining of these species." – The Galactic Council.

I started researching the idea that there had been other 'Batches' of humans that evolved on Earth. After praying, I came across the work of a chap called Graham Hancock and his observations of ancient structures and things around the world that don't fit conventional 'Scholarly' versions of ancient history. The more I read and watched his work, the more it seemed to confirm that there have been different advanced Civilizations on Earth. And that the timeline the 'official' story talks about, just doesn't make sense. 'Fingerprints of the Gods', his most popular book, is very compelling and makes a great challenge to the mainstream view. Almost demonized for his opinions by mainstream academics and branded a pseudo-scientist and pseudo-archaeologist. It seems clear that he is not pretending to be anything of the sort and is just pointing out the obvious. Like ancient maps that have a pretty accurate depiction of an Antarctic coastline, hundreds of years before we 'officially' knew there was one, should be taken more seriously. And challenging the absurd assumption that the great pyramid, a building of such massive size, almost perfectly aligned to true North, that's mathematical proportions are a scale representation of the Earth, that follows the precession of the equinoxes, as well as being built incorporating both PI and the golden ratio in its dimensions, could have been intended as a simple burial chamber for one man.

"The great Pyramid of Giza - is the most significant point on your Earth plane. It is a reminder of your merkabas and is a very powerful place. It is a dimensional portal and connects directly to Orion. There are many discoveries on your time frame that are ready to happen regarding the great pyramid at Giza." - The Galactic Council.

According to Mr. Hancock, his fascination with this subject began in Ethiopia. Where he was told by a monk about the Ark of the covenant being kept in a Chapel there. The dismissal of this as a possibility by academics, and the arrogant rigidity to even entertain this notion irked him and set him on the path he is still on today. A search for truth rather than just acceptance of official narrative. The keepers of the Ark take the position for life and they suffer what sounds like some form of radiation poisoning. Like this 'heavenly' box is an advanced power source that would seem 'godly' to a primitive people.

"Take all sources that have been laid before you and scrutinize them, no matter where they are from." – The Galactic Council.

After another prayer, I was led to Nassim Haremin's work. He too was talking about the Ark of the covenant in the seminar that I watched that was called 'Tetragrammaton – the most sacred knowledge on our planet'. He deconstructed the word Tetragrammaton, from the Bible, and suggested that an equivalent was 'Tetrahedron', the sacred geometry of the Merkaba. Following the story in the bible and the descriptions given as Moses left with his people and the Ark, he came to the conclusion that the Ark is a power source that belongs in the great pyramid. The dimensions mentioned in the bible coincide precisely to the 'Sarcophagus' in the Kings chamber.

"Scrutinize the history that you have been told, and come to the truth within yourself" – The Galactic Council.

This is not just about the possibility of a major power source being plugged back in for it's relevant purpose. It is about our consciousness being ready for us to hear the truth of what was encoded into ancient texts. And the masculine and feminine polarities coming into sufficient balance so that we can use this power safely, wisely and effectively. This is the whole point of the ring pass not. When our internal world is at peace and in a creative, rather than competitive focus, we break out of the cosmic egg and are endowed with the awareness to live with greater potential. The immense power that the Ark contains is an external representation and manifestation of the same power that can be accessed within us with our Merkabas'.

The Fermi paradox – Is the apparent contradiction between the massive size of the observable universe. The probability that there would be intelligent, developed life elsewhere. And the lack of evidence that there is any. According to astrophysicists, 1,000,000,000,000,000,000,000 or one sextillion, more than all the grains of sand in the whole world, many times over, is how many Suns there are in just the observable universe. Which seems to be a

staggering number. Until you realize that there are more than a thousand times more $H2O$ molecules than that in a glass of water. The micro and macro world, just our physical existence is mind-blowingly immense. But other dimensions and the idea of the Multiverse, whose supporters include Stephen Hawking, Michio Kaku, and Leonard Susskind, bring us a different understanding that may solve the Fermi Paradox. If the next stage in a species evolution, past the mastering of the elementary physical stage, includes the validation and tangible accessing of inter-dimensional travel. It is possible that the vast distances that need to be traveled in space for developed species to connect are traversed instantaneously. And we are being observed constantly.

"Truth is stranger than fiction, but it is because fiction is obliged to stick to possibilities; Truth isn't." – Mark Twain

The great pyramid is on an invisible line, like the equator, that perfectly circles the globe. On this line are many ancient, sacred spots. Easter Island, Machu Pichu, Angkor Watt, Cuzco, Petra and the list goes on and on of sacred sites that have pyramids or some spiritual significance. Many of them built on the remains of even older sites. Why would this be, if not them having a more profound purpose, a deeper connection - an inter-dimensional one. If these power points all connect energetically and the driving engine for them is the great pyramid. Once the power source is returned and the energy portal is reactivated, we will understand what global inter-dimensional travel is once again.

"You understand your position in your galaxy from what you have observed and analyzed. But the Earth is also an inter-dimensional ship that is capable of shifting its position. It has already done this several times. However, as it is just now, not being nurtured by your species, not being respected, not being loved the way it needs to be for the Earth Merkaba to be opened once again. The concentration of the Galactic Council and the members of your species ready to assimilate these concepts are of the raising of consciousness of mankind. Your Mother Earth needs your love right now and though the Earth will survive, she wishes you to survive as a species. All she

needs to help you is your love." - The Galactic Council.

The love that is required is already within us. But the Twin Flame reunion is vital at this time for the sparking of this power, this fire, this holy passion once again. Divine romantic love gives us courage, gives us peace, excites all of our tantric senses and motivates us to move mountains for our love, for our beloved, and for our destiny. Our beloved is actually within us, and the accessing of our innate divine power is helped by the searching for and finding of the Twin Flame. The power of the Twin Flame concept and fulfillment lies in wanting to be, and actively trying to be, a better person, not just trying to have the perfect partner.

"This is divine fire, purifying, golden, devouring all that is not love in it's path. This fire, now lit, will rage through the whole world until the task is complete. This fire will affect all." – The Galactic Council

The Twin Flame can never be lost because they are always within you. This is the biggest fundamental point that needs to be assimilated about this. And one that we were being constantly reminded of, even though we were together. "Detach, detach, detach" was my guides mantra. Not be cold or aloof, because genuine detachment is neither of those things. Real detachment is actually the greatest form of divine attachment. Because in detachment from the illusion or 'Maya', you are in complete flow, in complete mastery. You are in full trust that the divine is guiding you, empowering you, and awakening you into your fullest freedom. Giving you the power to be selfless. What seems like a great paradox is that true selflessness is actually the most self-serving thing. Because in the proper understanding of oneness, there is no other. What you do to the other, you do to yourself. So when you are living in surrender to divine will authentically. Everything is yours to love and all you experience in loving is reflected back to you immediately. That was why it was only when we had both let go of the concept of needing each other, that we were magnetically drawn together.

Love is the Drug got a hook in me

A lot of lightworkers dull the pain of their sensitivity with drugs. I certainly did in my formative years. And as a society, we are pretty much running on substances in general. The morning Psychostimulant cup of Joe to get us going in the morning is standard. Nicotine is still a biggy for many in spite of the knowledge of how exceptionally bad smoking is for us. A wee drink of alcohol to wind down in the evenings and weekends is expected. And the biggest one to me, though it is not classified as a drug, is sugar. We are a sweet-toothed people and are suffering terribly for it. This is not even generally seen as an addiction. Just the social norm.

The harder stuff is being used to deaden acute awareness. Many hard drugs are strong enough to take away this harsh reality completely for a time. Some of my childhood friends are no longer with us because of difficult habits. I was spared my life but I could have been having a much different reality.

"There are many who are going through self-deception and addiction who are trying to drown out the pain because they are Empaths. Sensitive to all around them, and the societal paradigms that you have put on each other, and put yourselves down as being weak. You do not want to show each other how weak you are so in your mental understanding you prove how strong you are through ingesting substances and laughing about it. It is this fear of ridicule and not wanting to be an outcast in your society that has caused many in your species to self-destruct. There are a myriad of different reasons but the main one is the disconnection to your spirit." – Metatron, this is the Healing Book.

Each different soul will learn their personal lessons about the recreational and social aspect of these things. We are never judged, in my experience, from the higher vibrational beings. They steer us in the right direction always. The cosmic high of transcending the dimensions in meditation and bringing that into waking experience is much more potent than anything I have ever encountered before.

Cannabis, when smoked, is carcinogenic, but when administered safely, is a healing gift from God. It is demonized and only now as prohibition seems to be ending, are we, as a society, starting to pay heed to the many studies that show just how important it is for our well being. Medicinally, most notably for MS, Parkinsons, Epilepsy, Anxiety and for pain relief. As an essential vegetable, it is a superfood that, when juiced, has a very positive effect on our health. The applications are numerous and when we harness its massive potential it has the ability to change many destructive patterns we are indulging in right now.

Lucy in the Sky with Diamonds could hold the key medicinally for a lot of ailments, from giving up smoking to treating depression, anxiety, and suicidal tendencies. Research in L.S.D is showing results that are amazingly positive. The Neuroscientist Dr. Robin Carhart-Harris believes that when we use psilocybin medicinally as a standard, that it will change the world in the way we treat psychiatric disorders. Instead of just "Taking the edge of things" with the mainstream treatments we use now.

Another drug that is catching the attention of the collectives ascending population is D.M.T. Many people are doing Ayahuasca ceremonies and having enlightening experiences with them. Dimethyltryptamine occurs naturally in our bodies in small amounts. We dream because of it and it is speculated that this is part of what the 'Divine Nectar' contains that the Galactic Council are talking about. Many have also suggested that it is this substance that is released when you go into a deep trance state. The spirit molecule is a documentary on the groundbreaking research done by Dr. Rick Strassman on D.M.T and is essential viewing.

"As you awaken your pure consciousness, coming to an understanding of your merkaba without the use of artificial stimulants or mind altering substances, you will be brought forward much quicker than those who transcend the dimensions with the use of additives. For the high that you can attain and the places that you can

go within your consciousness are much more powerful than anything that you can gain from any chemical enhancement. As you connect to the higher and higher dimensions, you will be able to do this consciously and the differing levels of bliss that you allow within your vessel, within your experience will bring you to a greater understanding of the expansion of your light bodies. If you follow to the letter the Clarion Call, your linear time frame of achieving ascension will be very quick." – The Galactic Council.

The problem with substances, with the goal of reaching higher states of consciousness, is the temporary nature of the experience. As you open your Merkaba, you can get the hang of accessing the bliss that comes into your waking state, even when you are not in deep meditation. The continual access to bliss is the very achievable goal of an opened Merkaba. It takes effort, but it's worth it. I'm not saying don't have a toke or don't spend some time with a shaman in a ceremony. What you do is up to you, and all experiences are valid in their own way. But if the goal is transcendence, meditation, to me, is the best advice. And opening your Merkaba is the gold star, fast express highway to your deepest reality.

What have you been smoking?

Would have been the question just a few years ago when talking seriously about E.T's or spaceships landing here. But the truth is we shall soon be in spaceships ourselves if Elon Musk and his contemporaries have anything to do with it. The reality of affordable domestic spaceflights is coming closer and closer. The Galactic Council are talking about us being able to take delivery of ships that are already here and all we have to do is raise our vibration. The excitement and reality of getting in a spaceship is helping accelerate our evolution. When the first cars appeared, it was only the elites that had them. That isn't really so long ago. We are soon going to be traveling in space by ourselves - one way or another.

I want it to happen before I die...

"You cannot die. You will have many more experiences of death, but that is all that they will be. You are eternal. You do not have to do anything to gain eternal life. There is no eternal suffering that you will have to endure for not succumbing to a scary story that was designed to control you by other humans. You are divine already. There is no judgment for believing in any of these stories either. Forgive yourself while you need that validation to feel better. But the need for forgiveness is only there until you allow yourself to embody your natural state of unconditional love. In the state of unconditional love, there is no need for forgiveness - because there is no judgment of anything that anyone does. The core of all experience is divine. God is the zero point. A blank canvas. To say God doesn't care is accurate. Not because of lack of compassion in the way you look at it from a human perspective. But because all experience is the gift from the divine to itself. Dark and light are needed to create form. It is all a big play and there is no meaning in and of itself. You are evolving to see that meaning is subjective and with ever-evolving perspective, meaning changes as you do. So any meaning is only what you give to it. The meaning of life is only ever to experience it. You gave yourself a limited perspective so you could have an experience of separation and then evolve back into your natural state of oneness."

As we are the product of many generations of beliefs that have been ingrained into our collective psyche, the benefit of protocols to bring us out of our amnesia and into our oneness is invaluable. That is what the Clarion Call, the Healing book, and the Galactic Council books are. They are protocols to bring us into our oneness. Because my personal, family tradition is Christian, they involve the language of that lineage.

"**The many different channels that are spreading the word of this truth are lighting your World up with more light than it has ever seen before. The darkness is failing, the negative is failing, but the positive naturally reinforces itself. Each one of you that step into your bravery, into your truth, into opening yourself up to the light, will strengthen the whole. The dark side fights against itself, but the light raises all others of light up and into the truth of love. Into the peace that passes understanding, to the higher truth that transcends all things.**" – The Galactic Council.

But the world is flat!

A growing movement is the flat Earth society. People that really believe space is just a conspiracy and that we are being lied to. The zeal that they have and the anger at anybody who challenges this belief is almost evangelical. Attacking simple scientific reasoning and sometimes stating that almost everything is a conspiracy. That the Government is corrupt and out to get us. That the Church is demonic and abusing its power. Why would there be such distrust? Why would 'Authority' be questioned in this way? Well, 'Authority' hasn't really done so well in the past as we are finding out with growing regularity. Churches, our moral 'example' have deliberately covered up vast multitudes of horrendous child abuse for decades as was illustrated in the Oscar-winning film 'Spotlight'. Wars are started on false pretenses by governments and millions of innocents are slaughtered as a result, as happened with the non-existent 'weapons of mass destruction'. We know all this to be true now, it's not a conspiracy theory. And the stress of this is creating lots of different reactions. The 'Official' story of many things being presented to us defies proper scrutiny. So it stands to reason there is a lack of trust. The flat Earth subject is growing because when we don't accept an 'Official' narrative that defies logic, the alternative is sometimes just as ridiculous.

Each different person will have their beliefs challenged as we move deeper and deeper into ascension. The closer we come to the critical mass, the closer we come mentally to the ultimate phase transition of **Mental Ascension**. After which, **Societal Ascension** will be at its next stage. Corruption will be replaced by integrity. Lobbying will be a thing of the past. The problems in our organizational institutions will subside and the trust will return.

"As soon as a critical mass of electrons are aligned within an atom – as soon as that single electron tipping point happens – you have phase transition, then all of the other electrons follow suit. Once there are enough of you that align to your divine consciousness and start to operate from it deliberately and consistently, all others of your species will automatically do the same. It will not be a struggle once that point has been reached. It will unfold as if a symphony was playing and the transformation of your world will happen on all levels in many different ways." – The Galactic Council

There are always two versions of yourself. Since I met Angelina this has been highlighted greatly. Each version can be changed at every moment. My weight problem has always been a way of me hiding myself away. I feel like I become invisible when I am overweight. I feel like a product of violent abuse and negative programming from my father when I am succumbing to this state. But the other state is confident, fit, charismatic and inspiring. A chap that can move mountains because of his own positive attitude and trust in the divine. This guy recognizes that my dad was just a fallible human that had his own problems. That he can do better than that and that the perspective he chooses will greatly affect the reality he experiences. This is the guy I want to be and the path that I want to follow. And I know that it is the direction of my own highest personal ascension. We all have our own vision of these two versions of ourselves. Ascension is consciously choosing this greater option for yourself. Forgiving the past, but deciding to do better.

"The defining moments of decision are what shapes your reality." – Galactic Council

Soon after we moved into the flat in Estepona, my sister-in-law Tanya suddenly passed away at the age of 46. This was a big shock and another wake-up call for me. I had known her since early childhood and it was a difficult thing to process. She was only a year older than me and the feeling that life had been far too short for her was very sad. I know that she is eternal and has just moved onto the next phase of her existence. But it brought into sharp focus the importance of appreciating every single moment we are here. I have not feared death since I first opened my Merkaba. But this temporary experience as Robbie will end, and, like most people, I don't know when that will be.

After praying for the next part of the book. I was led to stories of the three kinds of Rainbow death. A phenomenon that reportedly happens with advanced Tibetan Buddhist Yogi Monks. The first, and most common kind, which occurs every five years or so, happens after the monk dies. His body slowly shrinks to the size of a small child. Sometimes only hair and nails remain after the rest has dissolved into light. The second kind happens when the Yogi is still alive and the rainbow light can be seen while they go about their day. It can happen quickly over a week or sometimes over months or even years. In the final stages, the body shrinks to the size of a baby and then disappears in a flash of light. The third and rarest type is when the Yogi's body dissolves into light but stays visible, functional and transparent.

"Your body of light is the essence of your soul. The body that has been yours in all of your incarnations." – The Galactic Council

This process involves flooding the body with divine nectar. I was excited to read this as these cases have been documented from antiquity in the Dzogchen lineage. This means that the divine nectar that the Galactic Council are talking about is not just a brand new evolutionary addition to our body, but has been active for thousands of years. It is only the awareness of it that is being introduced to the wider humanity for **Spiritual Ascension**. These monks do a form of Yoga called Atiyoga with the end goal being the Rainbow body and 'Unexcelled wisdom'.

"You are Buddha's, you are all Buddha's. You are either sleeping Buddha or awake Buddha. Those who are awake see there is no problem, for all is perfect, all is just a reflection of the mind, all is just a reflection of the consciousness. And when you allow yourself to fully awaken, all you experience is the bliss of the Universe." - The Galactic Council.

The next place I was led to, after praying, was to an ancient sacred technique called the **Kechari Mudra.** This is where you curl the tongue up and touch the soft palate. As you continue practicing and go further with your tongue, you stimulate your pineal gland to help release the divine nectar. The writings on this coincide with what the Galactic Council describe. A loss of appetite and no need for food. Constant bliss and less need for sleep. More energy and divine buoyancy.

Although this has been practiced for thousands of years by dedicated yogis, masters, and avatars. You do not have to be someone that has spent their whole life meditating and cultivating purity to come into this state. **Spiritual Ascension** is the point where all of the deliberate spiritual work that has been done by our evolving ancestors and those consciously connecting to their divine core in the past, like these monks, comes to fruition within us as a collective. These monks are vegetarian and non-violent. A conscious choice that everyone on the planet can make right now. All you need for Ascension is purity of intention, an open mind, and an open heart. Love is the key ingredient. No particular religion or tradition in its entirety is sufficient. All philosophies are incomplete in their antiquated form. An upgrade is happening and a willingness to let go of the outdated software is important.

This is not to say abandon your heritage. It's an honoring of what our ancestors were trying to convey, but with bug fixes. The viruses of power abuse, dogmatism, misogyny, hypocrisy, fear, guilt, shame and self-aggrandizement cannot pass the ring-pass-not. And this is an individual ascension first. This starts with you.

"No matter what you do, do something, raise your vibration. For there is, in effect, what is becoming two Earths. It is what people discuss when they talk about moving into the fifth dimension. Although there will still be one physical planet. There will be two very definite points – those who have raised their vibration and those who have not. A caterpillar cannot go into its chrysalis until it is ready for its metamorphosis. As you are reading this, you are already in metamorphosis dear ones. We are excited to witness your transforming experience." – The Galactic Council.

Apocalypse Apathy Alert

If ten people were in a small room on an isolated base on the moon. And they had a machine that created enough oxygen for them to breathe. Then one of them tried to break the machine and start a fire that would burn up the rest of the oxygen. The other people would stop it, no question, right? We are in a finite biosphere on the Earth. We are burning fossil fuel at a crazy rate and If we don't have the trees and plants to absorb the Co2 and create oxygen, we will not survive. The Amazon is being cut down systematically for profit. The oceans, which provide most of our oxygen and transform a great deal of the Co2, is being polluted with all of the plastic waste. And the rise in temperatures means the phytoplankton, which is 70% of our oxygen machine, is dying. Forget so much about flooding, we can always live on boats. But we can't survive without breathing.

"Right now there is simply no need for you to pollute your atmosphere burning fossil fuels that you believe you must rely upon. The energy that surrounds you, that is within your planet and that is upon your planet is far greater and much safer than you are currently using. Once again it is only economics and the very small percentage of your population that benefit from the

current paradigm. They are not only keeping you cold in your winters but are draining your bank account unnecessarily. The technology to change this is already here. With the current projection of your collective mindset and the plans of your lower chakra selves in the oppression of your population, it will be fifty years before you are fully free from this boil that needs to be burst. However, with each one of you that joins the Galactic Council, that magnifies your potential and that opens up the new paradigm that frees you from the oppression and the fear dynamic, you shave time off the linear time frame. Raise your voices and come together in your inspiration and transformation." – The Galactic Council

When a system has proven to be detrimental to the whole and is having catastrophic effects on the biosphere with profit as its only concern, there has to be change, and it has to be quick. In **The Third Industrial Revolution**, Jeremy Rifkin has outlined achievable plans to change the global infrastructure from old worn out energy systems to renewable, sustainable and ecologically efficient ones. This is the practical application of **Technological Ascension**, with **Societal Ascension**. How we achieve this will have to be in cooperation with each other. The corruption and money interests must be overcome to achieve it. And this will take our **Spiritual Ascension** to raise consciousness so we stop impeding our own progress. The love we have for each other is the motivating force for making this change.

"Love sees no obstacles. It runs marathons, leaps chasms, breaks down barriers to achieve its goal. It never fails." - Metatron

The Twin Flame phenomena is happening right now because the amount of divine love flooding the planet needs to be grounded and expanded. Every person that opens to the love within, is expanding this experience. Each different relationship has the potential to expand spiritual awareness. We are all each other's Twin Flame in some ways because we are all one. The biggest lesson that we will ever learn in this regard is that fulfillment is never going to be given to us by anyone other than ourselves. The Twin Flame is within us and as we come to more reverence and love for each and every relationship that we have, the more we will see that reflected back to us. The search within us leads to the discovery outside of us.

When Twin Flames are fully sincere, in complete detachment, allowing the other the trust and freedom to err or rise at their own volition. And dealing only with their own connection to their divine core. It opens a gateway to spirit that frees the greatest amount of guidance from source. This state is full grace and a catalyst for all those connecting with them.

The deepest relationship can only happen when you are in full surrender to your divine purpose. We all have some purpose that the divine within is working through us to achieve. For some it is parenthood, for some activism, for others it is sports, entertainment, writing or traveling. Whatever it is that lights you up, that fulfills you, there you will see your Twin Flame. There you will find your mission and the way that your heart can open up fully.

The Law of Delusion

The law of attraction is very powerful and the understanding that we create our own reality is vital for the ascension of humanity. However, the delusional misunderstanding that if you just daydream your best case scenario randomly, that it will appear before you, has caused a lot of misery to students of this law. It is true that we can create anything that we can think of. But it is also true that we have given ourselves parameters that we are here to overcome and transcend. Within our material circumstances, as we think of a better case scenario, the universe jumps to it, to create what we positively believe can happen. The more we detach from the outcome, the quicker the way to achieve our vision is shown to us. But we must also take steps towards that manifestation. If we don't, we miss the chance to create. The old story of the minister on the roof of his church during a flood is the perfect illustration of this.

The minister was patiently waiting to be saved by God. A dinghy passed by and offered a lift. But the minister refused, saying god was going to save him. Then a boat passed by and offered safety. Once again the offer was refused. Just as the minister was about to drown, with the water surrounding him, a helicopter offered a final hand of hope. But the minister stood firm in his faith. Then he drowned. Upon arriving in heaven and facing his maker, he asked why God didn't save him. God replied "Well, I arranged a dinghy, a boat, and a helicopter. But you had your own ideas."

We don't want our Twin Flame. We want how that will make us feel. We want to be happy and fulfilled. The same with wealth, fitness or ambition to do, be, or have anything. We are not in search of just the experience, but how it will make us feel. The law of attraction teaching flips things around so that the feeling is the important thing. When visualizing whatever we want to create, we imagine it already being here with the associated feeling, and so the law of attraction is put in motion. But we still have to act upon the signs, inspiration, connections, and directions the universe brings us.

"We are what we think. All that we are arises with our thoughts. With our thoughts we make the world. Speak or act with a pure mind and happiness will follow you as your shadow, unbreakable." – Buddha

The more you open your Merkaba, the easier the manifestation process becomes. The deeper in bliss you dive, the quicker whatever you want can materialize.

"The law of attraction is much misunderstood. And it is true that with your thoughts you create the World. However, the reality you experience is dependent upon your level of vibration for how quickly you manifest. For at a lower vibration you are subject to other sentient beings vibration and creation. When your mental body is clear and when you have raised your vibration, you can create whatever you want. When you raise your vibration to the zero point of bliss, things are created very quickly in your reality." – Metatron, this is the healing book.

Before we do any more creating, it is a good idea to recognize what it is we have already created. Whatever circumstances you are in just now are of your own creation. Whether that is through allowing or deliberate manifestation is irrelevant. The state of our whole world is a reflection of the level of our collective consciousness and has manifested perfectly in line with that level. **Ascension** is about us becoming consciously aware of what we have created and why. Empowering ourselves and others to the truth of our immense power. And then deliberately transforming ourselves, which in turn transforms the world.

"You can only do as well as you know how to. But once you know what you are capable of, do what you are capable of." – Metatron.

The Twin Flames that are already together, beaming their love and dealing with their humanity are helping those looking and waiting. The more people that we open our hearts to, the quicker everyone will find what they need. Not everyone will be with their Twin Flame. Not everyone needs that experience. But those with that yearning, according to my guides, will not be disappointed. We are all unique and what lights up one doesn't light up another, so there is no single prescribed path for everyone. But there are fundamental truths for us all. We are all divine and have a massive capacity for love and fulfillment. We all have a toroidal field and a Merkaba, waiting to be activated. Those who have already opened theirs are naturally in service. Because they know that the time is now for the greatest show on Earth. That the time has come to spread our wings. The time has come to raise our game, to raise our consciousness and solve the problems that our lower self has given us.

"Your situation is unlike anything you have faced before. You must revolutionize your mindset and your actions and have the courage to be honest with yourselves about the way you interact with each other. You have reached the sufficient global tension necessary for pushing through the ring-pass-not to embody the full quotient of your power as a species." – The Galactic Council

Humanity is at a crossroads and we are squeezing ourselves dramatically on all fronts.

No matter whether you are in the Illuminati or government, Vatican or slum. Think of yourself as pious or poisonous, intelligent or dumb. We are all ready to awaken and there is no discrimination when it comes to the divine. We are loved equally and the choice is upon us to take up the gauntlet and transform our situation. We are all in this together. We have the technology to make this planet a magnificent place where everyone is cared for and the war machine can be transformed completely through transforming ourselves.

"You have the technology to transform your whole world completely with not one human left out. War is old consciousness. Your power in awakening will reassign

your resources appropriately with abundance for all beings as standard. This is inevitable for your species and is a matter of when, rather than if. Each of you has the ability to greatly speed up this process." – The Galactic Council

At the end of the film 'The Matrix', when Neo says "No", as the 'Agents' shoot bullets at him and he stops them with his mind. This is a metaphor for us saying no to the way 'Authority' has been telling us that we need to kill each other for our own safety. This is the rebirth of Neo after the kiss from his Twin Flame, Trinity. As he awakens from his death, he sees everything as it really is. As energy, connecting everything and is completely without fear. His abilities are complete and he assumes his place, unhindered by the controlling forces trying to subdue his humanity. Ready to show everyone a world without borders or boundaries, where anything is possible.

The prophecy of the return of the Christ is happening right now as we awaken to the innate divine energies within us. Jesus was 33 at his death and rebirth. We have 33 vertebrae and the kundalini rises up from our base to our 'Crown', which is the return of the King. The kingdom is within you.

"Whoever drinks of the water that I will give him shall never thirst; but the water that I will give him will become in him a well of water springing up to eternal life." – John 4:14

As we release the divine nectar from our pineal gland, we experience an Ego death, open our Merkaba, and become one with everything. When the flow happens and we pass through the ring-pass-not - this is the truth of being born again. This has been encoded into ancient literature and the prophecy was so powerful because it is an inevitability. It is only the interpretation of it that has been misleading. And now, as circumstances are dictating a necessity for this ability to be realized, we are becoming aware of it.

"This mystery has been kept secret for a long time, but

now it is being revealed. **God wants everyone to know this rich and glorious secret inside and out. Regardless of their background or religious standing. The mystery is that Christ is within you, it's that simple.**" – Colossians 1:26

The time has come for us to let go of fear and open our hearts to the divine love that will transform the world completely. The divine nectar contains more bliss than any drug or material possession could give you. The Galactic Council say this is physically possible for every person that is incarnated now with a human body.

Authority I give to you

Since my tooth was healed all those years ago. I have known that there are two types of 'Authority'. There are the control and organizational systems we have created as a collective that can be incomplete, corrupt and serve only the few. And there is divine Authority, which serves everyone and empowers anyone that aligns with it.

You can embody this Authority when you have a pure intent and surrender to its flow. But you cannot fool it into serving you without that purity of intent. If you try, you will be swiftly given an ego lesson. This is why the ring-pass-not is there. Because we are being called to advance and leave behind old patterns of behavior that do not serve us anymore.

"The 'seven deadly sins' or anything that inhibits your full power are stages of your growth and understanding. Each comes with their own lesson on your journey. You will keep repeating whatever part of them is necessary until you are ready. Once you choose to not participate in the lesson anymore, you will move on to other challenges and embody a greater amount of your power. The choice to actively improve and open your energy system means you are ready to discard the elementary parts of your human learning experience. And are starting to discover

just how powerful you really are."

Ascension is not a moral dictate. It is not a campaign for a belief system or a standpoint from a certain point of view. It is happening organically irrespective of ideology. There is no need to prove God to be true. The divine doesn't need a campaign manager. This is not an us and them scenario. This is an us reality. The different texts that have been encoded by our higher-self are becoming clearer now as we are ready to accept what we are capable of.

The offices of the Divine

According to Metatron, we can access all of this illusion when we use our consciousness effectively, and play the game the way we have set it up for ourselves. We have the opportunity to embody the different powers with our individual personalities. Each different president has a unique style and point of view. But they all have the same authority with which to act.

"I can guarantee this truth: Those who believe in me will do the things that I am doing. They will do even greater things." – John 14:12

Each different point of the flower of life matrix, when accessed with your Merkaba, holds a different empowerment as you embody the different stages. As you open your Crown chakra and operate from a place of unconditional love, you embody 'The office of the Christ'. As you detach fully from the illusion, and fully onto the divine, you embody 'The office of the Buddha'. As you cut the cords and feel the mighty warrior within you, you embody 'The office of Krishna'. What will you do when you are in that office? What will you create when you embody your potential?

There are no sides, no real them and us, there is only opportunity for advancement within the game. And the opportunity to have an experience of different perspectives. The illusion of sides is to facilitate growth and experience.

Laughter is key

When you stop taking yourself so seriously and lighten up about everything, life changes drastically. We have systematically programmed ourselves to be stressed, worried and in fear. Our mental constructs from the social programming of our fledgling consciousness are designed intentionally to keep us 'in our place'. To elicit a violent reaction, and lead us to conflict. This brings us into an emotional crisis to make us fearful, docile and controllable. So when we become aware of this pattern and take steps, guided by our internal divine 'Authority', we are empowered into **Societal Ascension** and the way is made clear before us.

Some of the greatest truth holders are the comedians. Laughter lifts you from your seriousness. It can slice deep into your ego like a samurai sword and destroy it to the core without you feeling any pain. The best of it can detach us from the ridiculousness of our quirks and contradictions and leave us in a heightened philosophical understanding of our shared humanity.

"There are many messiahs upon your planet. The Messiah is one who has flowered in their consciousness and is ready, open and willing to give themselves over to the emancipation of the Human race in this current batch of your evolution. Your Messiahs are your writers, your poets, your singers, your entertainers, and your comedians. Every different walk of life has your messiahs." – The Galactic Council

We are all children of the revolution of consciousness. We are right in the middle of it. And our clarity of mind and spirit is so powerful, when activated, that we have all we need to make this planet fit for our children at last and make our mothers proud.

"Do unto others as you would have them do unto your family." – The Golden Rule.

Once you know how much power you have, stop believing any disempowering, controlling conditioning or propaganda and claim your divine sovereignty, there is no excuse anymore. There is no bogeyman. Satan is powerless when you don't fear him. When you realize that you can summon all the forces of the universe at will and that **you are** the universe. When you understand the power of your Merkaba and recognize the true power of love. That love can transform you in an instant, **and then actually let it**. You will not fear any group or person that would try to oppress you. Once you understand the power within you to inspire and create and connect and transform - **there is nothing that will stop you.** And as you claim your power, you will start to shine the true light that is within you and attract the others that are here to do the very same. And for each of us brave enough to stand in our light, we energetically empower others to do the same. This knock-on effect is already happening. The divine fire is here and nothing can extinguish it. This has been coming for a long time and it has arrived. We are ripe, awakening, flowering, and transforming. No longer accepting disinformation without proper scrutiny. No longer accepting 'official' narrative that is bought and paid for. No longer accepting less from ourselves than we are capable of. The wave of love will continue to build and will become a massive tsunami that will wash everything clean. And we are here to surf the waves and have fun doing it.

"Nothing is more powerful than an idea whose time has come." – Victor Hugo

Our time has come and we are ready.

Thank you for taking the time to read my book. I am grateful for all of the support and goodwill that people from all over the world have shown me since releasing the Clarion Call and the other ascension books. I have great faith in each and every one of you. Since going on this spiritual journey, my life has become much more fulfilling and my hope for humanity has increased as I see the awakening happening. I am blessed to have my beautiful Twin Flame Angelina by my side as we both push towards fulfilling our potential. If you are with yours or searching for them, I hope this book has helped you.

No matter who you are, or what religion, family background, country or planet you are from. Part of you is me, and part of me is you. And we are both divine. So whatever part your soul has decided to play in this game, I am excited that we are in this play together. And once the curtain comes down, no matter how dramatic the show was. We will all enjoy the rap party together.

Addendum

I did a channelling recently for my New York group that mentions soul groups and has a reference to the 144,000. This has been mentioned a few times in my books firstly regarding D.N.A and then about those who are on the same 'Mission' as you if you feel your purpose is to raise consciousness. The concept is that 144,000 Light-worker souls are incarnated at this time. One thousand groups of 144 that are divided into 12 groups of 12. Within the twelve there are six sets of Twin Flames. Each person in the group that is not your Twin Flame is your Twin Ray, according to the channelling.

This is a state of awareness, a channelling. I am not trying to claim anything as an absolute truth. Each individual should discern their own personal truth on their path. I am not claiming to be a Guru or a Messiah. I have had many amazing things happen to me that I cannot explain with my rational mind and have tried to be as thorough as possible in describing my own personal journey. I know that the me at 20 would probably have scoffed at what I have described in this book. But I would not want to change him then. He had to go through the experiences he had to change his perspective. Each different experience and relationship you have has the potential to change the way you see, relate to and interact with the world. How much you use it to benefit yourself and the lives of those around you is entirely up to you.

Best wishes,

Robbie Mackenzie

Manufactured by Amazon.ca
Bolton, ON